Also by Emilio Bernal Labrada . . .

Getting Away with Murder—and Castro's Crimes—In U.S. Public Life

Murders and felonies committed and covered up over the last fifty years in the United States and Cuba by top governmental leaders, their heirs and successors, with vast international repercussions, some obvious and others not.   First edition published in 2012.

Asesinatos Impunes y Crímenes de Castro en la Vida Pública de EE.UU.

Spanish version (by the author) of the above book. Published in 2013.

Versión en español, por el propio autor del libro. Publicado en el 2013.

Good Usage Prevents Abusage / El Buen Uso Impide el Abuso

A bilingual exploration into difficulties, improper expressions, absurdities, and outright abuses committed by journalists, bureaucrats and everyday speakers against the top languages of the planet: English and Spanish.

To be published soon.

Exploración bilingüe de los entresijos, expresiones erróneas, absurdos y desenfrenados abusos que cometen los periodistas, burócratas y el común de los hablantes contra los primeros idiomas del planeta: el español y el inglés.

Se editará próximamente.

La prensa liEbre o Los crímenes del idioma

Colección de artículos y ensayos sobre desopilantes disparates espánglicos en la radio y teledifusión así como en la prensa, por obra y gracia de periodistas, burócratas, publicitarios e incluso traductores. Publicdo en 1999.

A collection of articles and essays about Spanglish howlers in broadcasting and print, committed by journalists, bureaucrats, advertisers and translators. Published in 1999.

Antología de Emilia Bernal: verso, prosa y traducción poética

Antología de la poetisa cubana en tods sus facetas. Selección e introducción del poeta, escritor y académico Manuel J. Santayana.

An anthology of the Cuban poetess Emilia Bernal: verse, prose and translation of poetry. Selection and introduction by the poet and writer Manuel J. Santayana.

Emilia Bernal: su vida y su obra

Biografía y obra—verso, prosa y traducción poética—de la poetisa cubana, por Armando Betancourt de Hita. Revisado, organizado y prologado por Emilio Bernal Labrada. Publicado en el 2001.

The life and works—poetry, prose and poetry translations— of Cuban poetess Emilia Bernal, by Armando Betancourt de Hita. Edited, organized and prefaced by Emilio Bernal Labrada. Published in 2001.

Antología de El trujamán

Selección de textos sobre traducción. Los artículos de Emilio Bernal Labrada, al principio del libro, se titulan: "Whitman: ¿tildado deególatra por traducciones deficientes?", "El tranvía erótico", *"Bahamas, Bermuda* y otros trastrueques caribeños", y "Excusas sin pretexto".

Selected texts on translation. The essays by Emilio Bernal Labrada, entitled as indicated above, appear at the beginning of the book. Papeles del Centro Virtual Cervantes – Madrid (Spain), 2002.

Al pie de la Casa Blanca

Este libro contiene una selección de poesías del autor como parte de una colección de versos debidos a la inspiración de poetas hispanos residentes en la región de Washington, D.C. Publicado por la Academia Norteamericana de la Lengua Española, Nueva York, 2010. (La versión en inglés aparecerá próximamente.)

This book contains a selection of the author's poems as part of a collection of poetry by a number of Hispanic poets who reside in the Washington, D.C. area. Published by the North American Academy of the Spanish Language, New York, 2010. (An English version will be forthcoming shortly.)

All books available from the author at emiliolabrada@msn.com, or amazon.com

TOP-SECRET   COVERUPS

Emilio Bernal Labrada

FIRST EDITION

September, 2016

Advance Reviews

After his breathtaking political thriller Getting Away with Murder...*, an exposé of heinous crimes at the highest levels of government, Emilio Bernal Labrada delivers yet another literary probe into that sinister world embellished by media hype, uplifting rhetoric, and mindless euphoria. Reappearing are some of the famous names already known to us, recognizable through suggestive spelling. But in this further instalment the author uncovers still more outlaws and unsuspected atrocities. In all, an exciting, revealing page turner by a writer-researcher at the top of his game.*

> Manuel Santayana, PhD   Author,
> translator, critic

In yet another historical novel—a sequel to Getting Away with Murder...*—the author has researched further atrocious crimes disguised as accidents, suicides, etc., while updating previous revelations. Upsetting established myths, he combines known facts into plausible conclusions, blowing away the smoke-screens conjured up by the culprits and their accomplices: i.e., self-interested media moguls, government officials, and other dissemblers.*

> Edward Keen
> Author, translator, critic

We are all familiar with the Borgias and other such ruthless schemers from the past. But the atrocities they committed, we've been conditioned to think, happened centuries ago. We now live in the best of possible worlds, as Leibniz would have it, and are infinitely more advanced. Top Secret Coverups*, however, tells a different story. Read it closely, but be warned: this is not for the faint-hearted!*

> Guido Mina di Sospiro,
> Author of *The Forbidden Book*, et al

I dedicate this book to the researchers who struggle, very often namelessly and at great risk, to bring to America the truth about its own history.

TABLE OF CONTENTS

INTRODUCTION

What strikes me about the author is that he is not only courageous, highly intelligent (a Mensa member) and a thorough researcher, but also extremely fond of his adoptive country: the United States of America. He is also clearly a staunch enemy of tyranny and a lover of freedom, most especially of speech, the press and information.

Why else would he take the risk of writing a book of this nature, taking on powerful individuals and families who have controlled the U.S. government for decades and maintained coverups that to this day remain official gospel, unchallenged by the press and by those in power? Perhaps more dangerously, this book defies the long arm of the tyrants ruling his native Cuba, a land that he can now not visit without putting on the line his life, or at the minimum risking imprisonment and torture—at his age, in his ninth decade, tantamount to a death sentence. But never mind that: take a look, in Chapter XII, at the crimes committed against America and democracy by these despots, who were no less than instigators and accomplices in the crime of the 20th century—the murder of JFK.[1]

When critics dismiss Bernal Labrada's research and chain of reasoning in debunking popular myths about heinous crimes, calling them "conspiracy theories", he has an answer: such theories arise only because the "official story" of an event is so far-fetched and unsatisfactory that it strains credulity to the breaking point. The scenarios he sets forth in this book are quite the contrary: rock solid.

---

[1] The assassination of JFK is dealt with at greater length in a previous book, *Getting Away with Murder—and Costra's Crimes—in U.S. Public Life*. This "sequel" provides further information.

His step-by-step weaving of each story, based on existing, accepted evidence, brings into play simple logic and common sense applied to known facts. Such are the cases that have haunted this nation over the last fifty years: assassinations pure and simple, frequently disguised as suicides, accidents or natural events beyond human control. But there is plenty more: **presidential rapes** (yes, you read that right!), **rigged elections** and **blackmail.** These last two powerful but unspoken crimes have shaped the nation's destiny far more than mere governmental policies.

The author further reasons that—as we have long suspected—the **blackmail** of JFK was the reason for the fiasco known as the Bay of Pigs, an intentional event that left Cuba firmly in the grip of Castro. Furthermore, it turns out that this very same tyrant "doubled down" by being an accomplice in the murder of his number-one adversary: JFK. This complicity and the conspiratorial knowledge thus gained created the shield that has ever since protected his unspeakable regime. *That* information, plus something else of a sexual nature involving a former first lady (and now, perhaps, president-to-be), enabled him to employ **yet more blackmail** in order to force the administration of her husband, four decades later, to commit an evil, cowardly deed. (If the same presidential couple, in a long-planned, foreseeable role-reversal, returns to the White House, they will again be subject to Castro's further extortion, a grim prospect for America and freedom.)

In sum, greed, evil, ruthlessness, thirst for power, despotism, unbridled sexual desire and plain human frailty have been at the root of the tragic, unspeakable events for which the United States has paid, and continues to pay, an unconscionable price.

Thanks, Emilio, for coming from Cuba to tell us truths that we Americans had all-along ignored or suspected—but were afraid to face.

Anonymous

AUTHOR'S PREFACE

I know, I know: I will be asked for "proof" of the rapes, murders, felonious crimes, corruption and wrongdoing described herein—never mind the misdemeanors. My answer: it is not my job to file charges nor, even less, to make them stick; far from that. I am neither a prosecutor nor in charge of any "official" investigation aimed at punishing the law-breakers. In any case, most of those involved—the murderers, rapists, felons, thieves, conspirators and their accessories and flunkies—are long dead and buried.

True, a few are still alive, as are uncounted relatives and descendants. They are all welcome to come after me. If they do their job carefully and properly they will make it look like an "accident" or "suicide" and they'll most likely get away with it. But that will only increase the distribution of this book and spread the true story that they, their forebears, contemporaries and descendants have so far successfully covered up. For me, the truth is far too important—as it should be for anyone—to worry about what might accelerate one's departure from this garden of earthly delights. At any rate, 90% (perhaps more) of my life is over and done with, so exiting before I use up the remainder of my journey is of minor concern.

I just think it's about time that someone came up with some honest answers about what really happened to the brothers Kennedy—John and Robert—, John Kennedy, Jr., Martin Luther King, Marilyn Monroe, Hugo Chávez, (the Venezuelan sorcerer's apprentice), Alfredo (Che) Guevara de la Serna (the Saint of the Americas), Lee Harvey Oswald (the self-described "patsy"), Jack Ruby (concerned about "sparing the Mafia-loving Kennedy family further grief"—yeah, right!), Sirhan Sirhan (another patsy), Jesse Burle Ray (yet another patsy), Jorge Mas Canosa (Cuban exile leader and the Castro brothers' worst exiled enemy, "taken care of" by their Russian associates), O. J. Simpson's ex-wife and her companion (their killer is still being hunted down by Simpson himself), and many lesser-known figures. Not to mention J. Edgar Hoover, the czar of his own personal Bureau—designed to investigate his enemies, that is, and cover up his personal crimes—and whose passing, an unpunished crime in itself, was a true blessing for which America should be grateful.

I also offer an honest, risky-for-me explanation of truly mysterious events such as: 1) the failure of the invasion at the Bay of Pigs (a mistranslation, by the way[2]), leading to the survival of the evil brothers Castro, 2) the use of blackmail by Castro to force the Clintons to return the child Elián González to the despicable Cuban tyranny, from which his mother had rescued him by paying the ultimate price (an act accomplished in an extrajudicial and utterly bizarre use of force), and 3) other uncanny events that still are head-scratchers to some, but become clear when the puzzle pieces form a perfect fit.

In effect, the American people have been, over the last half century, the victims of an extensive, compulsive and highly organized, top-down coverup, in which officialdom has engaged the support of a compliant, subservient press to keep the lid on the truth. The unusual foreign-policy and domestic events since 2010 have also been sheltered with shady rhetoric that falls far short of the facts and deals with superficial evidence while purposely skirting the underlying cause. But this period is too recent and complex to be subjected to an exposé; it would, in any case, require a separate book.

It's worth repeating that it is not my objective to provide judicial proof, but simply to bring to bear rational arguments and assemble a virtual jigsaw-puzzle. If the pieces fit, to paraphrase a well-known attorney in a famous case discussed in this book, you must convict. I refer, of course, to the court of public opinion—not to a jury of one's "peers" than can be swayed by emotional appeals and psychological hucksterism.

But I will let you, the reader, make up your own mind—a magistrate, each one of you, in the Supreme Court of Public Opinion.

---

[2] The word *cochinos* in the toponym *Bahía de Cochinos* refers not at all to swine, but to an indigenous Cuban fish known by that name.

CHAPTER I

Presidential Rapes and Sexual Harassment

Although many U.S. presidents have likely committed rape and similar felonies without ever being prosecuted or even charged, a couple of relatively recent ones come to mind whose criminal behavior has gone relatively unpublicized and completely unpunished.

JOHN F. KENNEDY, GENTLE ABUSER

One of the women involved with this president actually wrote a book, 50 years afterward, in which she described her experience in some detail. Since she was a virgin, the event was unforgettable and remained engraved in her remembrances. Even though she was kind enough to state that she did not consider it a rape—very considerate of the murdered president's memory—the truth is that if she had reported it and the man had not been the sitting Commander in Chief, he would most likely have been charged and prosecuted.

Suffice it to say that he did not take her out to dinner and a movie but simply led her on a tour of the White House and, when they got to his wife's private bedroom—she was nowhere near—he guided her down on the bed and proceeded to have his way. Too scared and impressed to offer any resistance, she passively acceded and went on to maintain a relationship of sorts with him for a year or so.

Kennedy's affair with her began in 1962, although she met him briefly a year before, in 1961, when she was a senior at Miss Porter's School in Connecticut and was editor of the boarding school's intramural publication. Hoping to interview the most famous alumna of the educational institution, Jacqueline Bouvier (by then Mrs. Kennedy), she asked for and did get an invitation, except it was only to visit the White House and talk to Lillian Dandridge, the First Lady's social secretary.

While there she felt fortunate and thrilled to briefly meet President Kennedy himself. He no doubt made a note of her beauty because a year later, while a freshman at Wheaton College in Massachusetts, she was surprised to be offered a job as a White House intern, even though she had never even applied for it!

"I was excited about this job. It seemed like a miracle," Mimi said. "I was a little bit wide-eyed I think, not knowing exactly what to expect, but full of enthusiasm and hope."

Although all of her story cannot be verified (some protagonists have since passed on) NBC News has talked to several JFK administration people who have confirmed that she was indeed a White House intern and seemed to enjoy special access to the president. An oral history by a White House aide at the time, Barbara Gamarekian, refers to "Mimi" (she went by that nickname), a beautiful intern whom she suspected was having an affair with Kennedy.

Initial Encounter with the President

Thus hired, Marion "Mimi" Beardsley (her full name), a debutante from a prominent New Jersey family, traveled to Washington in the summer of 1962 and was assigned to the White House press office. Only four days later, JFK aide Dave Powers came by and invited her to go for a swim in the White House indoor pool.

"A group of us are going to have a swim at lunchtime. Would you like to join us?'", Dave Powers said casually, she recalls. "I think I was probably so taken in by being invited to go do it that I didn't think too much about it." Even though it seemed odd, she did not stop to question such an irresistible offer. "I'll just go ahead and do it", she concluded.

Mimi says she was joined by two other girls in the pool, White House staffers Priscilla Wear and Jill Cowan, playfully dubbed "Fiddle and Faddle", who made her feel comfortable. That was quite clearly a part of their job.

"Shortly after that, the president arrived. So I was sort of surprised that the president was joining us. No one had said the president was going to join us, but he went and put on his trunks and came into the water", she recollects. After the swim with the president they all went back to work.

Let us quote from Mimi's book: "It didn't seem unnatural. It sounds funny to say that, but it really didn't seem unnatural, just because everybody was friendly and this is what we were doing and I went back to work afterwards. No one said anything." (Years later, calls to Priscilla Wear to confirm the story were, as expected, ignored.)

A few hours after her first swim with the president, Mimi received another call from JFK aide Dave Powers, now inviting her upstairs to the White House residence for a new staff welcoming.

"There was a pitcher of daiquiris on the coffee table and Dave [Powers] poured me one", she recalls. Since it was the first time she'd tasted a daiquiri, it likely put her at ease. "And then the president arrived," she goes on. "He sat down, very relaxed, put his feet up on the coffee table and sort of joined in on the conversations.... Obviously these were the people that he liked to relax with and then there was I, which seemed a little odd, but I didn't think much about it."

Mimi says that Kennedy then approached her and asked if she wanted to take a private tour of the rooms his wife had recently redecorated. "There was nothing in my mind that thought anything other than what I was being offered which was a tour of what the White House looked like", she explains.

Kennedy then took Mimi on the tour and, on arriving at Jackie Kennedy's bedroom, "I felt the president getting closer and closer to me," Mimi said. "His way didn't make me nervous and he came close, very close, and looked me right in the eyes and I actually, he then put his hands on my shoulder and sort of guiding me down to the edge of the bed, sort of the corner of the bed and I think he may have even said to me, 'Is this all right'...I don't really think I knew what he was talking about."

Mimi further explains that she was a virgin who had only gone as far as kissing a boy when she was in eighth grade. "Obviously what did happen was I lost my virginity right there. Then, I think I went a little bit into shock," Mimi said. "He kept asking me if I was all right and I was all right, there was not a lot of conversation."

In this memoir of hers, Mimi recounts that Kennedy "maneuvered me swiftly and unexpectedly and with such authority and strength that short of screaming, I doubt if I could have done anything to thwart his intentions."

Decades later when Mimi confided in friends and family, some wondered whether she what Kennedy did was rape.

"I don't consider it was rape. I don't," Mimi said. "If I had said no, I think the president would have stopped, but I didn't..... There was no coercion."

A few days after her first encounter with Kennedy, Mimi says she was invited again to meet him in the private floors of the White House. "I had just a little bit of second thoughts, not enough to keep me from going back," she said.

This was a pivotal point in her relationship with Kennedy, Mimi says, marking it as the beginning of what she considered their secret affair.

Cooking with the President, Hairdressing and Bathtub Games

In Marion Beardsley's recollections of her sexual coming of age with Kennedy she refers to them as full of variety and fun; for her, he was a sensualist who at times liked to be completely silly, particularly in the bathtub.

"He had a collection of little yellow rubber ducks and they were in the bathtub and rubber ducks became sort of part of the game," Mimi said. "We had races with rubber ducks in the bathtub. I know he was not being president when he was with me." She adds that Kennedy showed her how to cook eggs in a double boiler, which was the way he liked them. At times they listened to records.

"I think maybe I reminded him of a younger time in his life," Mimi said. At one time she even learned how to do a perfect coiffure for him through special hair treatments.

"I ended up taking care of the president's hair. He had that wonderful hair and it always needed to be in great shape and so I learned how to do the head treatments," Mimi said.

Mimi says that she sometimes dressed his hair in the Oval Office itself. During her internship she would sometimes spend the night at the White House, but discreetly enough so that no one took notice, or at least pretended not to.

"Secret Service might have known, but nobody ever talked to me about it," Mimi said. On occasion she traveled with the president, but on the support plane in her role with the press office. On one trip to California she took part in a large party at Bing Crosby's home. That was likely the one originally scheduled for Frank Sinatra's place in Palm Springs, that the president was persuaded to switch away at the last minute—because of Frank's Mafia connections—. This provoked a lifelong split between Sinatra and Lawford, whom he blamed for the snub, as well as a definite cooling of Kennedy's relations with the singer.

But of course Mimi was unaware of all that and enjoyed herself. "It was exciting. It was glamorous, it was fun", she says in her book. However, during many trips with the president she admits that often she had to "play the waiting game," spending hours in a hotel room waiting for him to get away from his scheduled activities to visit with her.

"I should have felt guilty. He was married to Mrs. Kennedy, but I didn't at the time feel guilty because I think I felt this closeness to him," Mimi said. Looking back now, the former intern realizes that she was at the beck and call of the 45-year-old president.

"I can see it's not a good place for a 19-year-old to be in a relationship that's so imbalanced and with such a powerful person and an older man and at [his] beck and call", Mimi adds. "I see how sad it was."

Kennedy Asks Mimi: "Take Care" of Powers, Brother Teddy

Looking back, While Mimi says that while the president made her feel special, he had a "dark side." The most disturbing incident occurred at the White House pool, Mimi says.

While Mimi and Kennedy swam one day, presidential aide Dave Powers sat at poolside. Little did she know that, as it has later been revealed, Powers was the go-to man in charge of procuring young, attractive women for his boss; in recognition, the president occasionally made him the beneficiary of their favors. In this case that is apparently what took place. According to Mimi, Kennedy whispered in her ear that Powers looked tense and asked her if she "would take care of it'. Mimi writes in her book, "I knew exactly what he meant. Take care of it. That was a challenge to give Dave Powers oral sex. I don't think the president thought I'd do it, but I'm ashamed to say that I did."

Mimi showed her emotions when telling her interviewer that the incident still makes her sad and angry. "It makes me angry because I didn't just splash water in the president's face and tell him to get lost", Mimi said. "It makes me sad because I did it."

JFK aide Powers died in 1998, before Mimi came forward with her secret. Mimi goes on to say that, on another occasion the president also asked her to "take care" of his brother, freshman Senator Teddy Kennedy. Since that time she refused, it likely accelerated the end of their affair.

Pregnancy Scare and Cuban Missile Crisis

After her returning to college in the fall, she briefly panicked that she might have become pregnant and told Mr. Powers about it. "He said that he would put me in touch with someone who would put me in touch with someone who would put me in touch with someone down the line if I should need help and luckily I didn't," Mimi said.

Once that was over with, she and the president continued their liaison even though she was in college and it involved some traveling on her part. They devised a pseudonym, "Michael Carter", which he would use when calling her dorm.

When nothing else worked, the president would breezily arrange to bring her back to the White House. One of these occasions involved the tense night just before the Cuban Missile Crisis was resolved. "I think the president wanted me to be there," Mimi declares. "I really didn't spend much time with the president. I was just there." Unsurprisingly, she claims that they did not sleep together that night.

In the summer of 1963, Mimi returned to the White House as an intern once again. Since she was responsible for photo sessions in the Oval Office, she saw the president almost daily. However, perhaps because of the pregnancy of First Lady Jackie Kennedy—whom she never met—her own access to the president after hours was more limited.

Kennedy only brought up family matters with Mimi after the sad death of his newborn son, Patrick, in August 1963.

By October, Mimi had fallen deeply in love with a college student she'd been dating since earlier in the year, Tony Fahnestock, to whom she had not confided her affair with the president. When they became engaged, Mimi says Kennedy congratulated her. "He was happy for me and sort of joked that, 'Oh, well, you're not going to leave me are you?' So it was a kind of complicated thing for me, but he was happy that I had met Tony."

Kennedy gave her as a special present two gold pins with diamonds in the center, plus an autographed picture with a note, "Warm regards and best wishes and appreciation." He joked that what he was really appreciating her for would be their secret, Mimi says. Once engaged, the dynamics of her relationship with Kennedy shifted to friendship rather than sex.

The Assassination Uncovers her Secret

The last time they saw each other, Miami says, was at the Carlyle Hotel in New York City, on Nov. 15, 1963. He gave her a wedding gift of $300 and promised to call on returning from Texas. Seven days later Mimi heard the devastating news with her fiancé as they drove to his family's home in Connecticut.

"I could hardly breathe. I was in so much pain," Mimi writes. "Here was Tony who I was going to marry, who I loved, there was the president who I had loved, who I had spent 18 months with, he was dead. The feelings were just explosive inside me."

The excessive grief stunned her fiancé, who became curious about what might have been going on between the two. So she broke down and told him about the secret affair that no one else had ever heard about.

"Tony's reaction was emotionally violent," Mimi writes. "His response was so devastating that at that moment what happened for me was I just shut down emotionally... because what Tony said to me was, 'you and I will never ever talk about this and you are never to tell anybody else'."

She simply shut down her emotions and vowed to bury the secret forever, making a special effort to forget her experience and never mention her summers as a White House intern on resumes. She even got rid of the gifts Kennedy had given her, cutting up the autographed picture of the president and pawning the gold and diamond pins. Not telling anyone for so long was very hard, she stated.

After she married Fahnestock in 1964, in a similar twist of fate, Mimi lost her first baby to the same lung syndrome that had taken away Patrick, the president's son. She did, however, go on to have two healthy baby girls.

Turnaround, no Regrets

According to her book, Mimi's emotional shutdown impacted her marriage to Fahnestock, and they eventually divorced. Still, she doesn't regret the affair. "I don't actually regret that I had the affair with President Kennedy. What I regret is that I was shut down emotionally," Mimi said, telling her interviewer that she is sorry she did not let her parents know about the relationship. "I think they died not knowing all of me," she said.

The story of this particular affair of Kennedy was first mentioned in 2003 when historian Robert Dallek, in a biography of Kennedy, referred to a beautiful intern who was believed to be one of his paramours at the White House. When the New York Daily News tracked her down, Mimi submitted a written statement acknowledging the affair, but did not speak publicly.

Shortly after the story came to public attention, she met her future and current husband, who was not at all affected by it. On the contrary, Mimi says his encouragement helped her deal with the past and write her memoir.

Knowing there would be critics, she went on to say: "People are going to judge me. There's nothing I can do about that. All I can say is that, for me, to write this book, *Once Upon a Secret*, was extremely important. I had to do it... I can't separate the Kennedy name from it. This was part of the story."

Mimi was quite clearly not the only White House intern, secretary or employee whose favors President Kennedy enjoyed; she was only one of many and was likely well aware of the situation. Knowing what we know today about him—despite still being idolized by the press—he probably used the same modus operandi on many other young women impressed by the power and prestige of his high office.

However, few women, particularly later on in life when they have raised a family and maintained high standards of respectability, have the courage to bring up such matters, let alone write a book about them. In this case, it took 50 years to summon the will to do so.

Therefore, we are unlikely to learn of more such tales about Mr. Kennedy. Our next story, however, is much more profusely populated by events that, somehow, have never to this day gripped the public imagination. Why is an unfathomable mystery, considering the public information available for decades on his behavior, which as we shall see was, and perhaps is still, far more abusive and serious.

WILBUR J. CLANGDON, SERIAL VIOLATOR

Numerous women have come forth and complained about being molested and forced to have sex with this well-known compulsive womanizer, before, during and after his two terms as president. So many, in fact, that the term "bimbo eruptions" was coined to "explain" and brush off what was going on with considerable regularity during his terms as attorney general and governor of his state, and later as president.

Since his days as a Rhodes Scholar at Oxford 40 years ago, women have been accusing Bill Clinton of sexual assault. A continuing investigation into the President's sexual history has brought up incidents going back to his college days. That we know of, over a dozen women have claimed that his sexual appetites took no cognizance of rejection or denial.

From 1978-1980, during Clinton's initial term as governor of his state, troopers assigned to protect him learned of complaints from women who said Clinton forced himself on them or attempted to. A retired state trooper said in an interview that a common jocular remark among his protective squad was "who's next?" Another one stated that after political events they would often escort women to his hotel room, at times more than one per evening.

Former FBI agent Gary Aldrich wrote in his book *Unlimited Access* that when Clinton left Oxford University for a "European Tour" in 1969, he was informed by University officials that he was no longer welcome there. Aldrich said Clinton's academic record at Oxford was lackluster. Although he did not complete his studies at Oxford, Clinton later obtained a scholarship at Yale Law School. The State Department official who investigated sexual cases involving Clinton said his interests appeared to be drinking, drugs and sex, not studies. "I came away with the clear impression that this young man was there to party, not study," he said.

The following are among the known and documented cases of sexual abuse by Clinton.

Eileen Wellstone, an English 19-year-old, reported that Clinton sexually assaulted her shortly after they met at a pub near Oxford, where the future President was a student in 1969. A retired State Department employee, who asked for anonymity, confirmed that he interviewed the girl's family and filed a report with superiors. Clinton admitted the sexual encounter, but claimed it was consensual. In any case, the victim's family declined to pursue the case. In 1972, a 22-year-old woman told campus police at Yale University that she was sexually assaulted by Clinton, a law student at the college. No charges were filed, but retired campus policemen contacted by Capitol Hill Blue confirmed knowledge of the case.

The woman was tracked down by Capitol Hill Blue and confirmed the incident, but declined further discussion and denied permission to mention her name. In 1974, a student at the University of Arkansas complained that Clinton, her law school instructor at the time, tried to keep her from leaving his office after a conference, groped her and forcibly fondled her breasts. When she complained to her faculty advisor, Clinton claimed the student "came on" to him.

The student, who quit the school shortly thereafter and returned to her home in Texas, confirmed the story but declined to put it on the record. Several former students at the University confirmed the story in confidential interviews and said there were other reports dealing with his attempts to force himself on female students. In an interview with Capitol Hill Blue, a retired State Department employee said he believed the story told by Miss Wellstone. "There was no doubt in my mind that this young woman had suffered severe emotional trauma", he said. "But we were under tremendous pressure to avoid the embarrassment of having a Rhodes Scholar charged with rape. I filed a report with my superiors and that was the last I heard of it." Miss Wellstone, who is now married and lives near London, confirmed the incident when contacted this week, but refused to discuss the matter further. She said she would not go public with further details of the attack. Afterwards, she changed her phone number and hired a barrister who warned a reporter to stay away from his client.

Juanita Broaddrick, an Arkansas nursing home operator, told a female NBC TV reporter (reportedly Lisa Myers) that she was raped by Clinton. But NBC filed the interview away, saying they were confirming all parts of the story, until finally deciding to broadcast it. Broaddrick, however, finally took her story to The Wall Street Journal, which published her account of the brutal sexual violence at the hands of the future president; this story was then taken up by The Washington Trumpet and other publications. The White House did not return calls for comment. White House attorney David Kendall has issued a public denial of the Broaddrick rape. But Capitol Hill Blue confirmed that Broaddrick's story is only one account of many attempted and actual sexual assaults by Clinton that go back 40 years. The details of the attack on Broaddrick, which took place in 1978, are as follows.

Although for years rumors circulated about the Broaddrick encounter, she refused to discuss it with the media and submitted an affidavit to attorneys for Paula Janssen declaring them to be without foundation. However, in an interview with NBC's Dateline on February 24, 1999, she stated that Clinton had actually raped her.

Clinton met Broaddrick during his 1978 gubernatorial campaign, when he visited her nursing home and she volunteered to help. Since he invited her to stop by the campaign office in Little Rock, she got in touch a few weeks later while there for a nursing home conference. Explaining that he would not be in the campaign office that day, Clinton first suggested they meet at her hotel's coffee shop and then requested that they adjourn to her room to avoid the reporters gathered in the lobby.

Speaking briefly in her room, he described plans to renovate a prison visible just out the window if he won election. Broaddrick stated that, with no preliminaries, Clinton then suddenly kissed her, at which point she pushed him away, telling him she was married and not interested.

As recounted in an NBC interview, she went on to say: "Then he tries to kiss me again. And the second time he tries to kiss me he starts biting my lip ... He starts to, um, bite on my top lip and I tried to pull away from him. And then he forces me down on the bed. And I just was very frightened, and I tried to get away from him and I told him 'No,' that I didn't want this to happen but he wouldn't listen to me. ... It was a real panicky, panicky situation. I was even to the point where I was getting very noisy, you know, yelling to 'Please stop.' And that's when he pressed down on my right shoulder and he would bite my lip. ... When everything was over with, he got up and straightened himself, and I was crying at the moment and he walks to the door, and calmly puts on his sunglasses. And before he goes out the door he says 'You better get some ice on that.' And he turned and went out the door."

When asked if there was any way Clinton could have thought it was consensual, Broaddrick stated: "No, not with what I told him and with how I tried to push him away. It was not consensual." According to the legal definition, the last anyone heard, *nonconsensual sex* is equivalent to *rape*.

Broaddrick shared her hotel room with her friend and employee Norma Rogers, who said that after attending a conference seminar that morning, she returned to find Juanita on the bed "in a state of shock," her pantyhose torn in the crotch and her lip swollen as though she had been hit. According to Rogers, Juanita complained that Clinton had "forced himself on her." She then helped Broaddrick ice her lip, after which the two left Little Rock. She added that Juanita, very upset on the way home, blamed herself for letting Clinton in the room.

Juanita Broaddrick says she did not tell Gary Hickey, who was then her husband, what had happened, but explained that she had accidentally injured her lip.

At the time she was in a relationship with her eventual second husband, David Broaddrick. When he inquired about her injured lip, she simply told him that Clinton had raped her. Two friends confirmed that Broaddrick had told them the same thing at the time: Susan Lewis and Jean Darden, Norma Rogers' sister.

Although she did not recall the precise date of the event, Broaddrick said it was the spring of 1978 in the Camelot Hotel. Records show that she did indeed attended a nursing home meeting at the Camelot Hotel in Little Rock on April 25, 1978. Although the Clinton White House did not respond to requests for Mr. Clinton's official schedule for the date, news reports indicate that on that date he was in Little Rock, with no official business engagements in the morning.

Three weeks later, Broaddrick attended a Clinton fundraiser at a local dentist's home. She said she was "in denial", feeling guilty and thinking that she had given Clinton the wrong idea by letting him into her room. On her arrival a friend who had picked the Clintons up from the airport told her that his wife Hillary had asked if she would be at the event. Broaddrick says Mr. Clinton did not speak to her at the venue, but Mrs. Clinton approached her, took her hand, and said 'I just want you to know how much Bill and I appreciate what you do for him." When Broaddrick moved her hand away, she says, Mrs. Clinton held on to her and said "Do you understand? *Everything* that you do." Broaddrick says she promptly left the gathering, nauseous at the realization that Mrs. Clinton had clearly issued an unequivocal threat that she remain silent about what happened in her encounter with her husband.

About six years later, Broaddrick's nursing facility was judged the best in the state, which brought a congratulatory official letter from the governor. On the bottom was a handwritten note from Clinton, saying, "I admire you very much." According to her account, in 1991 Clinton called her out of a state nursing-standards meeting to attempt an apology, anticipating launching his 1992 presidential campaign. In response, as she told The Washington Trumpet, "I told him to go to hell, and I walked off". Someone who also attended the meeting said that Broaddrick was seen talking to Clinton in the hallway.

Further Public Disclosure

Though Juanita Broaddrick was very reluctant to go public, rumors began circulating at the time of Clinton's 1992 presidential bid in 1992. Broaddrick did confide in Phillip Yoakum, a friend from business circles.

When Clinton won the Democrat nomination, Yoakum, widely considered to have a Republican agenda, contacted Sheffield Nelson, Clinton's opponent in the 1990 gubernatorial race and arranged a meeting with Broaddrick. However, she resisted Yoakum's and Nelson's urgings that she go public. Yoakum secretly taped the conversation and wrote a letter summarizing the allegations, which began to circulate within Republican circles. The story reached the New York Times and the Los Angeles Times in October 1992, but the papers dropped the story because Broaddrick refused to talk to reporters.

In the fall of 1997, Paula Janssen's private investigators tried to talk to Broaddrick at her home, also secretly taping the conversation. However, she declined, saying "it was just a horrible, horrible thing," and "wouldn't relive it for anything." Although the investigators warned that she would likely be subpoenaed if she remained reluctant, Broaddrick insisted that that she would deny everything, saying "you can't get to him, and I'm not going to ruin my good name to do it... there's just absolutely no way anyone can get to him, he's just too vicious." Even though she was actually subpoenaed in the Janssen suit soon after, she likely committed perjury by submitting an affidavit denying that Clinton had made "any sexual advances." The recording of Broaddrick's conversation with the investigators was leaked to the press, but Broaddrick continued to refuse to speak to reporters.

In a case of this nature, one has to assume that powerful forces were brought to bear to keep the case as much under wraps as possible: in the event that "stick" did not work, a juicy carrot might have also been brought into the picture.

Despite Broaddrick's denial in her affidavit, Janssen' lawyers included her name and Yoakum's letter in a 1998 filing, suggesting that Broaddrick's silence had been bought; this was made more explicit by describing a phone call in which Broaddrick's husband said that he intended to ask Clinton "for a couple of big favors" and asked Yoakum to deny the incident. Along with the discrepancy between the letter and Broaddrick's affidavit, this attracted the attention of the presumed "independent counsel" Kent Star, who was investigating Clinton for obstruction of justice. Approached by the FBI, Broaddrick consulted her son, a lawyer, who gave her useful advice. Accordingly, she recanted the affidavit only after being promised that she would not be prosecuted for perjury for her affidavit in the Janssen case. However, she still insisted that Clinton had not pressured or bribed her in any way, and so Star felt free to disregard the matter in his investigation and referred to the matter in a mere footnote.

Those acquainted with the Star investigation have always maintained that the Attorney General at the time carefully selected him knowing that she could rely on him to "go easy" on the Clintons. Which is precisely what happened.

But back to our story. Though the mainstream media was not interested, rumors continued to circulate in tabloids and on talk-radio mentioning Broaddrick, who was upset by allegations that she had been paid off. She therefore agreed to an interview with NBC's Lisa Myers on January 20, 1999, the day after Clinton was impeached. However, the interview was broadcast 35 days later, after Clinton had been acquitted in a clever and still unclear political deal. Fingers were pointed at NBC for intentionally sitting on the story and applying exacting standards of corroboration until the impeachment process was over. It was clear that NBC had gathered the key corroborating evidence within 10 days of the interview, even though an assistant producer said it might have taken 14 days. In any case, that time frame would still have brought up the matter during the impeachment.   In conclusion, the incriminating story was delayed until it was no longer relevant, i.e., after the impeachment was over.

Other Cases

Carolyn Moffet, a legal secretary in Little Rock, said that after meeting the governor at a political fund-raiser in 1979 she received an invitation to visit his hotel room. "I was escorted there by a state trooper. When I went in, he was sitting on a couch, wearing only an undershirt. He pointed at his penis and told me to suck it. I told him I didn't even do that for my boyfriend and he got mad, grabbed my head and shoved it into his lap. I pulled away from him and ran out of the room."

The former Miss Moffet has since married and left the state. When she told her boyfriend, who was a lawyer and supporter of Clinton, he advised her to keep her mouth shut. "He said that people who crossed the governor usually regretted it and that if I knew what was good for me I'd forget that it ever happened," she said. "I haven't forgotten it. You don't forget crude men like that." Like two other women, the former Miss Moffet declined further interviews. A neighbor said she had received threatening phone calls.

Elizabeth Ward, the Miss Arkansas beauty who won the Miss America crown in 1982, told friends she was forced by Clinton to have sex with him shortly after she won her state crown. Last year, Ward, now married and using the surname Gracen (from her first marriage), told an interviewer she had sex with Clinton but labelled it consensual. However, according to close friends of hers she maintains privately that it was not, and that Clinton used force.

Paula Corbin, an Arkansas state worker, filed a sexual harassment case against Clinton after an encounter in a Little Rock hotel room where he exposed himself and demanded oral sex. Clinton reportedly settled the case by paying her $850,000 in cash.

Sandra Allen James, a former Washington, DC, political fundraiser says that when Clinton was running for the presidential nomination he invited her to his hotel room during a political trip to the nation's capital in 1991, pinned her against the wall and stuck his hand up her dress. She says she screamed loud enough for the Arkansas State Trooper stationed outside the hotel suite to bang on the door and ask if everything was all right, at which point Clinton released her and she fled the room. When she reported the incident to her boss, he advised her to keep her mouth shut if she wanted to keep working. Miss James has since married and left Washington. Reached at her home later on, she commented about later learning that other women suffered the same fate at Clinton's hands when he was in Washington during his Presidential run.

The staff of Capitol Hill Blue, a Washington publication, spoke with the former Miss James, the Washington fund-raiser who confirmed the encounter with Clinton at the Four Seasons Hotel in the nation's capital, but said she would not go public because those who do were being destroyed by the Clinton White House. "My husband and children deserve better than that',' she said when first contacted. After reading the Broaddrick story, however, she called back and gave permission to use her maiden name, but advised that she had no intention of pursuing the matter. "I wasn't raped, but I was trapped in a hotel room for a brief moment by a boorish man", she said. "I got away. He tried calling me several times after that, but I didn't take his phone calls. Then he stopped." But Miss James also retreated from public view after other news organizations contacted her.

Christy Zercher, a flight attendant on Clinton's leased campaign plane in 1992, says presidential candidate Clinton exposed himself to her, grabbed her breasts and made explicit remarks about oral sex. A video shot aboard the plane by ABC News shows an obviously inebriated Clinton with his hand between another young flight attendant's legs. Zercher said later in an interview that White House attorney Bruce Lindsey tried to pressure her into not publicizing the assault.

Kathleen Willey, a White House volunteer, reported that Clinton grabbed her, fondled her breasts and pressed her hand against his genitals during an Oval Office meeting in November, 1993. Willey, who told her story in a 60 Minutes interview, became a target of a White

House-directed smear campaign after she went public. In an interview with Capitol Hill Blue, the retired State Department employee said he believed the story told by Miss Wellstone, the young English woman who said Clinton raped her in 1969.

Many of the above encounters have been confirmed by numerous interviews with retired Arkansas state employees, former state troopers and former Yale and University of Arkansas students. Like others, they refused to go public because of fears of retaliation from the Clinton White House.

Monica Lewinsky. A 22-year-old White House intern, she was just the type that Bill Clinton regularly preyed on. Their "affair" went on for about two years before it came to public notice. The case is the one best known since it led to the President lying under oath and an impeachment process that Mr. Clinton's forces derailed by a last-minute deal that saved his presidency. Although this relationship appeared to be consensual, one must take into account the asymmetrical situation of an extremely powerful man and a very young, inexperienced girl, 19 at the time, hoping for a career in government.

An interesting note is that Clinton never consummated their "affair", settling for sessions of oral sex. Having gone that far, Monica was of course open to maintaining regular sexual relations, but the president remained reticent, explaining that such a step would have "consequences" and bring complications.

As a result of this scandal and the resulting impeachment and trial, President Clinton was penalized by suspension of his license to practice law in his state, a decision later upheld by the U.S. Supreme Court, and was fined $90,000 for giving false testimony.

During the course of this process, widely covered in the media, the press accused and upbraided itself for providing excessive coverage(!). When asked to comment on the subject, Mrs. Clinton had no complaints about her husband; instead, she defended him by saying that he had been the target of a "vast right-wing conspiracy" since the beginning of his political career. She proffered not a single critical word regarding his behavior—neither with respect to her personally nor about his outright lies to Congress and the press. Furthermore, she made no reference to his mendacity nor to the numerous other cases—that we know of—in which her husband used and abused women, nor did she express any sympathy for his victims. Her only complaint had to do with his enemies' "conspiracy": **that** was the cause of his troubles, not his own deeds.

It should be noted that, in the Paula Janssen case, Miss Lewinsky submitted a sworn affidavit denying a relationship with President Clinton. Although this might have subjected her to prosecution for perjury, no charges were ever filed nor even discussed, that we know of.

If so, her defense might have had to do with pressure from her boss. At any rate, the Lewinsky affidavit was delivered to Kent Star, the Independent Counsel who was investigating Clinton on multiple other matters, among them the Whitewater scandal, the White House FBI Files affair, and the White House Travel Office matter, in which staff were unfairly dismissed.

Conclusions and Reactions—by the Public and the Press

An interesting sidelight is that wide reporting of the Lewinsky scandal—to be expected from a free press—led to criticism of the media for excessive coverage. One wonders who could have considered that unjustified and begun to blame them for doing their job.

Still, serious journalists and writers persevered and looked into the president's questionable conduct. *Uncovering Clinton*, and *No One Left to Lie To*, books by Michael Isikoff and Christopher Hitchens, respectively, established the credibility of the Broaddrick case, pointing out its similarities to the modus operandi in the sexual harassment of Paula Janssen, which came up years later.

Clinton's Fatherhood Brought into Question

A number of details in Broaddrick's account dovetailed with allegations brought up by other women. Among these was Elizabeth Gracen, who stated that, in an apparently consensual encounter with Clinton, he got excited and also bit her lip. Afterward, he told her that there was no danger of pregnancy from him since he had been sterilized by mumps in childhood. Another of Clinton's well-known lovers, Jennifer Flowers, confirmed that he never used protection because he believed it impossible for him to make a woman pregnant.

Although such personal matters might normally be out of bounds, the fact that public figures are involved makes it important to bring up this point: the inescapable and consequential question of who fathered Mrs. Clinton's daughter, today a woman with children of her own. Rumor has it that since Mrs. Clinton has had affairs of her own, particularly with attorneys who worked with her in Arkansas at the Rose law firm, she might have conceived the child as a result of one of those relationships. Obviously, her husband must have accepted the circumstances and agreed to bring up the child as if he were the biological father. Considering his conduct, she of course deserves no censure for having had her own affairs—with both men and women, as has been widely reported. But, does not personal conduct, sexual or otherwise, have something to do with integrity, honesty and responsibility in "public servants"?

What quite clearly emerges from all this is that Mr. Clinton, with the ready, willing and able support of his wife, has managed to avoid, dodge and slip out of all these highly sensitive matters reflecting on his own and his wife's honesty and integrity. Part and parcel of this incredible story has been the reluctance of the press to pursue the matter, which it otherwise has done against others guilty of far less, tirelessly investigating cases and bringing them to public notoriety and scorn, if not actual national humiliation and legal consequences. We recall one president who was forced to resign.

Further questions not asked by anyone are extremely troubling. Has the press been suborned, threatened, or both? Why has the matter of Mrs. Clinton's own amorous activities been off limits during the decades that this husband-and-wife team has been dominating the political scene? It should be kept in mind that by teaming up with her spouse in their public life, Mrs. Hillary Clinton has been able to pursue an immensely profitable career—loaded with power, perks and huge expense accounts—in politics and government, as an outcome of which her husband might enjoy another term or two in the White House with all its privileges—and none of the responsibilities. The public seems unaware of the fact that spouses in a position of public power such as the presidency share a great deal more than a bed: they share the use of public property, salary and expense accounts, and make transcendent governmental decisions together. Therefore, is that not practically equivalent to being in office beyond the legal two terms?

As of this writing it is public knowledge that the Clintons have become enormously wealthy, having accumulated several billion dollars in a foundation that actually bears their surname. But is it really separate and apart from their personal fortune?

Mrs. Clinton's Judgment

This brings up the troubling question of whether Mrs. Clinton's judgment is trustworthy, considering just three of her recent actions and statements. First, a public comment that she and her husband were "flat broke" when they left the White House. Second, and equally disconcerting, was this remark at a congressional inquiry on the Benghazi attack that resulted in the death of our ambassador and four other diplomatic staff: "At this point, what difference does it make?" (This makes no sense when the whole point of an inquiry is to find out what happened and who was responsible.) Third, the use of a private server for her official e-mails. (A blatant breach of official protocol that implies, at least, extremely poor judgment and disregard of national security.) Some have wondered if the private email server was an attempt to keep private and secret any deals or transactions between foreign entities and the extremely rich Clinton Foundation. Others point out that she wanted full control of her communications and did not want State Department officials to access them. Either way, it reeks of an egotistical attitude that manifested little concern for security, whether national or for individuals that might be involved.

Cases not Made Public

What has become public knowledge about Mr. Clinton's predatory habits with respect to women indicates that there might be many more such cases that are still unknown and, with the passage of time, are unlikely to be brought up. What we know might be, as the saying goes, only the tip of the iceberg, since those who get away with crimes and misdemeanors get into the habit of doing them serially and only reduce their activity temporarily when there is danger of detection. Generally, they not only perfect their technique, but also learn how best to keep their deeds covered up through bribery, threats or both.

In conclusion, what else is there that is still unknown and remains to be discovered by the public?

It goes without saying that readers should make their own decision as to giving Mr. and Mrs. Clinton any more access to public funds, facilities and privileges, let alone any national and international powers and responsibilities.

HERMIONE CLANGDON, Enabler, Accomplice and Protector

It is quite clear that Mrs. Hillary Clinton has been aiding and abetting the predatory and criminal behavior of her husband since their marriage some 40 years ago and throughout his political career. Her personal interests were clearly served, since her ambition was to eventually become president of the United States. It seems safe to say that her motive in marrying him was largely based on the fact that, in her incisive perception, this skilled womanizer, as a high elected official, had the potential to achieve the presidency: i.e., *her* ultimate goal. He was quite clearly a popular, vote-getting politician at a time when women were still not accepted by the public as national leaders of such stature. And she had gotten nowhere as a volunteer in the Barry Goldwater Republican campaign as her first step in politics. As soon as she met Bill, she realized his possibilities and changed parties.   As of that moment she became a willing and able accomplice in covering up his multiple affairs, which she—bright and knowledgeable—must have become aware of from the very beginning. Consequently, she felt entitled to some of her own, which she is reputed to have actively pursued with men *and* women. And why would husband Bill object since she was his accomplice in his own relationships? They likely chose to accept, enable, abet and cover up each other's extramarital adventures.

Did Husband Bill Father the Child they Raised?

This brings up a delicate point. As indicated above, the child they supposedly had together is said to not be biologically her husband's, but fathered by another man who is supposedly friendly with them to this day. This tends to be supported by the fact that, as Mr. Clinton has often claimed to his paramours, he is unable to induce pregnancy as a result of mumps in childhood. As a factual matter, it is also true that none of his numerous sexual partners have ever filed a paternity suit against him, even though he apparently has never used any protection. This, by the way, may have well been the reason that, on occasion, he is said to have contracted certain STD's.

Bill's Defender in Publicized Cases

As the record shows, Mrs. Clinton has come out time and again in defense of her husband during so-called "bimbo eruptions", i.e., claims by various women that they have: 1) been forced, coerced or seduced to have sexual relations with him, or 2) been subject to sexual harassment.

One major and sensational case was that of Monica Lewinsky, which resulted in Bill Clinton's impeachment for lying about it, claiming he "did not have sexual relations with that woman". He attempted to justify his statement by fudging on the definition of the term "sexual relations", but still had to answer to Congress for it and escaped a guilty verdict thanks to a last-minute political deal behind closed doors. Hillary Clinton remained supportive of her husband throughout the scandal. In an appearance on NBC's "Today" show she said: "The great story here for anybody willing to find it and write about it and explain it is this vast right-wing conspiracy that has been conspiring against my husband since the day he announced for president."

Since there was physical and recorded evidence that Mr. Clinton had for two years maintained the affair with this White House intern about which he lied—not to mention numerous other relationships, sequentially or simultaneously—the real point was his proclivity to engage in this behavior. If anyone conspired, it was he and she, and not political opponents; they simply realized what he was up to and called him on it.

Later on Mrs. Clinton used her status as his wife as a base for rising to political prominence, becoming a) senator from New York—with no legislative accomplishments to speak of—and then b) in 2008, a leading candidate for the presidential nomination. Her failure to achieve that objective, and fence-mending by the new president, gained her the position of Secretary of State and thus a launching pad for another try at the Democratic nomination in 2016.

Women's "Advocate"?

Hillary Clinton has lately become a flag-waving advocate of women's rights and their proper place in society and politics. But as history shows, she hasn't always been that concerned or considerate of her gender.

First, as indicated above, she has been the accomplice and protector of her husband in his treatment of women as sexual objects to be used and discarded at will.

Furthermore, it turns out that she was the lawyer for defendants charged with rape in the state where she later married the future governor and president. The victim in the 1975 sexual abuse that was Mrs. Clinton's first criminal defense case, has since spoken to the media only once. She discussed the matter briefly with a reporter in 2008, during Mrs. Clinton's first presidential campaign effort.

In a long, emotional interview with a local paper, the victim stated that Mrs. Clinton, a young but clever lawyer at the time, intentionally lied in court documents and went to unheard-of extremes to discredit the evidence submitted. In addition, she was recorded when making callous statements acknowledging the truth and laughed about her attackers' guilt. Both of these points are evidence of poor judgment and dishonesty. The recordings, from the 1980s, were unearthed by a publication named The Washington Free Beacon and made public. However, the general press has never picked up on it, apparently determined to bury it so as to not hinder her undying ambition of becoming president.

"Hillary Clinton took me through hell," the victim said at one point. Another publication that ran a story about the case agreed to withhold the woman's name out of concern for her privacy as a victim of sexual assault.

Vulnerability to Blackmail

Last but by no means least, Mr. and Mrs. Clinton are practically in the pocket of the Castro-family Mafia who control Cuba and use it as a base to take over other countries and, furthermore, aid, abet and commit acts of terror internationally. As a matter of fact, Cuba was on the list of terrorist countries until the Obama administration mysteriously decided to remove it, asking for no proof nor anything else in return.

Why are the Clintons subject to blackmail, you ask? Please refer to Chapter X, about the case of Elián González, a matter being decided by the judicial system when the President took unilateral action to kidnap by brute, armed force and return him to the Castro tyranny. Such action brings up the distinct, unmistakable scent of skullduggery; in this instance it was the use of blackmail to force an immediate resolution contrary to law, due process and human rights.

As indicated in that chapter, it is the proverbial "slam-dunk" that the Castros own a videotape of Hillary Clinton in a **compromising encounter** with a top female Cuban diplomat, the release of which for public consumption would be extremely embarrassing, if not positively lethal for the presidential couple, notwithstanding the recent relaxation of rules about extramarital behavior. It is well known that the Castros, as indicated in Chapter VI, "The Bay of Pigs Double-cross", regularly use bald-faced threats, if not bribes or both, to win practically every single battle they have ever engaged in.

Now, how would America fare in any sort of dispute or negotiation with the Cuban dictators under such conditions? The question answers itself: we lose before the first word is spoken or the first chip is put on the table. The deck is absolutely stacked against us. And that might also apply to any other international problem in which the tyrants might have a stake. It is well known that they have made a special "anti-imperialist" deal with Iran and can also use their puppet governments in Venezuela and other countries to exert tremendous leverage. Even though the latest "deal" with Iran is ridiculously one-sided on the face of it, things will get much worse when the Iranians conduct their first nuclear test or at least evidence of having such a weapon. Together with North Korea, we will then face *two* dangerous enemies with atomic weapons.

To be honest, a President Clinton, be it Hillary or Bill—it's all the same—would be an utter disaster for America and the forces of freedom throughout the world. We may know what to expect before this book is published.

Unfortunately, the alternative to the Clinton couple seems to be just as unpalatable to America. So we are faced with a case in which none of the choices are desirable. If Donald Trump were actually a Trojan horse he could not possibly do a better job than he is doing: easily losing the election.

CHAPTER II

The Kennedy Brothers and Their Conspiratorial Enemies

This story has already been detailed in my book *Getting Away with Murder—and Castro's Crimes—in U.S. Public Life,* but it bears retelling due to new information that has since come to light and to this author's attention.

Let us deal only, insofar as possible, with the actual crimes, leaving the extraneous details, prequels and sequels aside. On the face of it, the story is seemingly so far-fetched that to this day many refuse to believe it, choosing to put their faith in a fairy tale so absurd that only small children would accept it as credible.

First, an unknown individual, acting alone with a cheap, old, mail-order, inaccurate rifle fires a series of shots in record time and kills the President of the United States. Then, 48 hours later, a Mafia soldier shoots the presumed killer, silencing him forever. The excuse cited by the Mafia soldier: to save the Kennedy family the agony of a trial and attendant publicity. Yes, of course! The Mafia has always been concerned about saving their enemies from grief; they're known to be extremely soft-hearted!

It has come to light that certain foreign leaders—one of them Charles de Gaulle, then French president—upon learning of the events concerning the assassination and subsequent murder of the suspect Oswald, recognized immediately that the official story was sheer poppycock and stated so privately.

But let's get down to some facts. President Kennedy had made himself serious enemies: the CIA, the FBI and the Secret Service—precisely the agencies entrusted with keeping him safe. In hindsight it is difficult to understand why he was so careless—er, the word is *overconfident.* But since the Kennedys had triumphed over every single obstacle, won every single battle and brazenly gotten away with all sorts of shenanigans, misdemeanors and crimes plain and simple, they likely considered themselves invincible.

The CIA's responsibility was to protect Kennedy from foreign threats, while the FBI and the Secret Service were in charge of warding off domestic ones; particularly the Secret Service. His most dangerous enemy abroad was Castro, who was already on the record publicly with threatening to kill him. Having learned of Kennedy's orders to have him taken out, Castro spoke publicly to the effect that, conversely, America's leaders could also expect to be targets for elimination.

Yet his most dangerous enemy was inside his own household, so to speak. More specifically within his administration. His name was

Lyndon Bernard Johnson. Out to become president of the United States since childhood, LBJ would stop at nothing in his climb to the top. Some had wondered, in 1959, why a man so powerful as the Senate Majority Leader would want to give up that position for the vice presidency, a job in which he would be a powerless second-fiddle to an upstart that he actually despised: John Kennedy.

In hindsight, the picture becomes clear: he wanted to reach the top and his time was running out. Either he got on the ticket with JFK or his goal would remain forever unreachable. The vice presidency, on the other hand, would put him one step away from the top spot. He was a cool calculator and knew that, based on family history, his life expectancy at the time was about 15 years (presciently, he had almost exactly that lapse left). That period could easily be eaten up by the youthful Kennedy family. LBJ's Mafia contacts told him that Kennedy was a sure thing; the Chicago boys would for sure take care of Illinois plus a couple of other states: enough to seal the victory. A deal had been struck and the Mafia never failed. Why, how else had Harry Truman "upset" Dewey when all the polls had the New Yorker well ahead? (Yes, you read that right: that's exactly what happened: the electoral results were rigged because of the Mafia's fear and hatred for Dewey, their implacable prosecutor/persecutor). Just for insurance, LBJ himself would make sure that in his own turf, Texas, the results would go into the Democratic column.

In brief, the Kennedys would be in and Johnson's only chance, after his defeat in the primaries, was to grab the vice-presidential spot: he needed only a foot in the door. Johnson, whose rise to power and prominence had been pure rocketry, sensed that he was now a small but major step away from his goal. All he had to do was play his cards right. JFK had already chosen a running mate: statesman-like senator Stewart Symington. But Johnson figured that he still had a chance. He arranged a face-to-face meeting just before the ticket became official and brazenly blackmailed Kennedy, threatening to expose his numerous pre- and extra-marital sexual liaisons with spies, prostitutes and other women who might present national security risks. All of this he did regardless of his own similar but more-discreet behavior.

Kennedy could have called his bluff but caved like a house of cards, even though his family and his whole camp begged him to stand firm. No one trusted or wanted the corrupt Texas politician. Some in the press speculated why a man who virtually controlled the U.S. Congress would give up such power for the vice-presidency. It just did not make sense. Ah, but it occurred to no one that there was an unspeakably evil and violent plan behind a move like that; perhaps no one wanted to think of the possibility that LBJ had *something*—more than the vice-presidency— up his sleazy sleeve.

Against the advice of his family and staff, JFK felt compelled to drop Symington like a hot potato—he was forced to call him and offer apologies. Johnson was the last man the Kennedy forces wanted as a running mate, but JFK could not face the dangerous alternative.

As became more in evidence later on, JFK was weak when it came to standing up to threats and blackmail (not the only such president, as we have shown: see Chapter X - The Elián González Case). Kennedy's well-known overpowering lust for women made him vulnerable, and in those days that was a cardinal sin. Thirty years later a certain Arkansas governor, who thought of JFK as his hero and probably topped his record of seductions—not to mention likely rape (see Chapter I)—got away with what back then would have wiped out anyone's political career.

Exactly as LBJ suspected, Kennedy was weak and readily gave in, perhaps consoling himself by thinking that he would keep LBJ at arm's length and find a way to get rid of him come re-election time. In retrospect, the decision cost him his life and the abrupt end of the incipient Kennedy dynasty. For the moment, JFK consoled himself with the thought that, once his first term was over, he would kick out LBJ and put his brother Robert on the ticket, thereby establishing a long-lasting Kennedy dynasty. LBJ was only a stop-gap measure to ensure this first step toward the family goal. His dad and Clan Patriarch, Joseph P. Kennedy, was already rubbing his hands in joyful expectation. He insisted that once John was in power, younger brother Robert be named Attorney General. The expectation was that he would do an outstanding job and earn his place on the next ticket, amid the respect and acclaim of the American people—all of that despite the fact that he had zero experience as a lawyer and was generally disliked as an impudent jerk. But the dynasty had to go strictly according to chronological birthright, just like royalty.

To implement the Kennedy plan against LBJ, the Justice Department, under Robert's own direction, started investigating him for corruption. The Vice President was to be indicted and forced to resign, bringing about the Kennedy-Kennedy ticket. In case that smacked of excessive nepotism and the country balked, Plan B was to have Robert run for president after John, with a discardable vice president, completed his second term. By then LBJ, the corrupt Texas politico, would have been disgraced, his career over; he might even have landed behind bars.

However, LBJ was an old fox and was not about to allow that. His spies in the Justice Department told him about the plan and urged him to act swiftly. All too clearly, he remembered his grandmother's words:

"that kid will wind up in the penitentiary". His reply was always the same: "I'll show 'em—one day I will be president".

Sure enough, as would become evident in due course, LBJ would not be deterred. He had shown that throughout his career, and awareness of his life expectancy would not allow any more time—even if it had, he was in no mood to wait. Thus, the die was cast and he proceeded to work on his scheme. After his ticket with Kennedy won (a cinch, based on his own and the Kennedy family's contacts and skill at electoral fraud), all he had to do was make sure something happened to the man in the Oval Office. To top it all he was thirsting for revenge, having felt disrespected by the Kennedys and their coterie of bright, cultured, high-society acolytes and admirers.

Only a Texas hack he might have been, but he would show them some smarts they would never forget. LBJ had the unusual ability to put together highly complex plans and apply clever, roundabout tactics to exert influence on top-flight personalities and achieve difficult objectives by threatening, cajoling and bribing—it was called "the Johnson treatment". He thus accomplished results that most ordinary individuals could hardly imagine. He was an expert at taking advantage of the nation's grief at Kennedy's death and maneuvered Congress into passing a vast amount of civil-rights legislation that *he himself had previously stalled*. Thus he got ample credit for it; although early in his career he had not been a civil rights advocate, his turnabout was not motivated only by a sense of justice and humanity: he saw the black voting block as a powerful force and thirsted for it. In his own words, he "ensured the black vote for the Democratic Party for 100 years". In short, Johnson was a doer and achiever, and he was far less concerned about methods than results. He could get away with the most outlandish schemes and come out smelling like a rose.[3] No wonder he had become Senate Majority Leader and a leading figure of his party, now very close to his goal of getting to the very top.

LBJ did not have to search far for allies in his plan to inherit the presidency. The Mafia, for one, noting that Kennedy had given them the double-cross, willingly hopped aboard. They concluded that the deal they had struck with the Irish family, through the Patriarch himself, Johnathan P., had been nothing but a cheap trick. Robert, their worst enemy since the Kefauver anti-organized-crime hearings, was on the warpath against them in no uncertain terms, and now as Attorney General, no less. There was bad blood between them and, contrary to the Mafia's expectations, it had not been washed away when they rigged the election and handed victory on a silver platter to JFK. Very shortly, the

---

[3] This brings to mind an LBJ quote : "I want 'em to kiss my ass and say it smells like a rose."

Kennedy administration evidenced that it was proceeding against the Mafia with all guns loaded and firing.

It was a shock. So much, that they at first came close to shooting it out among themselves. Some capos wanted to order a hit on Frank Sinatra, who had been the Kennedy standard-bearer to the extent that he even organized the inaugural celebrations, with personal appearances by huge stars—except for Sammy Davis, Jr., whose color made them uneasy and was about to marry a white woman. But enter Sam Giancana, Sinatra's bosom buddy—they had matching pinky rings to symbolize their close friendship. Sam came forth and said that *he* had also been duped by the Kennedys. Bumping off Sinatra, he said, would not fix anything; at any rate, their buddy the movie star had acted in good faith, and their job was to settle accounts with the *real* culprits and straighten out what had gone wrong. Shortly, reason prevailed and the capos calmed down, beginning instead to bond together to "take care" of the double-crossers.

When Johnson's feelers reached out to them there was common, solid ground: they had the same objective. He would keep, in spades, the promise that the Kennedys had breached: he would lay off. The Mafia, already planning to get even, realized that joining forces with LBJ was their ticket, without requiring so much as a nod. Johnson, they knew, was just as crooked as they were, per the old saying, "there is honor among thieves". They trusted each other.

Johnson's job now entailed enlisting co-conspirators at or near the top in the agencies in charge of the president's safety and of national security itself, foreign and domestic. The first item on Johnson's agenda was getting Hoover aboard. No problem: the FBI chief was a Kennedy hater and readily indulged in all kinds of skullduggery. Having Hoover would be the key to then approach the top men at the CIA and the Secret Service. Once he could say that Hoover was in, the other two would likely join. CIA Chief Alex Cullen should be happy to do so, having taken the rap and been fired for Kennedy's mishandling of the Bay of Pigs invasion. Cullen was made the scapegoat and Kennedy had intemperately said he would "break the CIA into a thousand pieces". Surely, they would be doing the country a favor by getting rid of such a chief executive and replacing him with a stronger, more reliable and sensible one: Johnson himself.

Once these two—the FBI and CIA heads—were aboard, the Secret Service chief, Koch, would be in the bag. The first two were well acquainted with each other and LBJ would know how to sway Koch. The Secret Service was unhappy with being in charge of procuring women for Kennedy—an improper and unlawful function that, to boot, affected national security and left the door open to blackmail (as we know, JFK was weak and open to it). With his skill at persuading and convincing,

LBJ felt the conspiracy plan should be in the bag, or well on its way. What better achievement than getting the top officers of the three agencies—FBI, CIA and Secret Service—to come aboard?

* * * * *

The complicity of Castro in the assassination of his worst enemy, JFK, is a fact little known by the public, although the top levels of the U.S. Government have long been aware of it. They have been careful to make no mention of it, since that would bring about all kinds of revelations and complications that they would rather not face.

Historically, the Infidel Castro has been the most **dangerous and longest-lasting tyrant in human history.** First, he used minimal forces—a guerrilla group of a few thousand that "overthrew" an established military force 50 times larger if army, navy and air force plus national police are combined. In fact, there were few actual battles: the government's forces were psychologically defeated and gave up, in part because eventual defeat seemed inevitable in view of America's withdrawal of support for the Batista regime. Castro's triumph in the face of such astronomical odds made him seem a man of destiny. Faith in him soared religiously and he became nearly sacrosanct. The people believed every word of his fake pro-democracy speeches. He was, if anything, an Oscar-winning actor posing as the ultimate God-given savior of the Cuban people.

Cleverly parlaying this popular wave of confidence in him, he gradually gained control of every single area of public and private life, political, social and economic. Step by careful step, he did the opposite of what he had promised and enthroned himself as an autocratic ruler and utterly, purposefully destroyed the advanced, prosperous society he encountered, while efficiently exploiting its human and natural resources to expand his reach abroad as a modern imperial power.

By the 1990's he had turned Venezuela into a Cuban colony, while Nicaragua and Bolivia, among other nations, became subservient and fell within his area of influence. Furthermore, even though he has not been the titular head of state for about a decade, he is considered an untouchable elder statesman and his word and will are still law. Popes come and go and pay homage to him and his regime, showering them with respectability. His exercise of virtually absolute power, since January 1, 1959, has at this writing reached a record-setting longevity of

57 years and counting. No other tyrant in human history has ever come even close. In practical terms a hereditary monarchy, the island of Cuba is under the implacable rule of King Castro, his brother, children and other family members. A clever and ruthless player, he has managed to outsmart everyone, starting with his country's own people and plowing through the Americans, the Russians and a large portion of Hispanic America, not to mention Angola, Ethiopia, and other areas of the African continent. He has also made powerful allies: for example, Iran in the Middle East, plus China and North Korea in Asia.

But, now that the we have set the stage, let's get back to our story. A most interesting sidelight that U.S. administrations have pretended to ignore has been his role as accomplice in the plot to murder U.S. President John F. Kennedy—an objective at which he succeeded with total impunity.

In brief, he recruited the U.S. Mafia to do the job. Initially, even before Kennedy became president, the mob was hired by the CIA and assigned the job of killing Castro. But it was not to be. Castro's super-effective intelligence service had excellent sources and, through pluck and luck, protected him at every turn. His agents had infiltrated not only the CIA and other American intelligence agencies, but also the Mafia itself. As a result, Castro was able to keep tabs on what was going on and stay ahead of the game. As a result, he soon discovered that powerful boss Santo Trafficante had come back again to Cuba—he was a frequent visitor, partly for amusement, to oversee the gambling business, and to get away from U.S. government agents. Castro had him jailed and demanded, in addition to ransom, special cooperation in intelligence, plus Mafia complicity in a certain highly secret operation he was planning.

Using this leverage and offering a substantial monetary reward as well, Castro enrolled the Mafia in the conspiracy to assassinate Kennedy. The Mafia gladly accepted since it was already collaborating with top U.S. officials to do precisely that. Castro likely suspected their involvement in the conspiracy, but wanted a) to buy "insurance" for the deed and b) to become privy to the American assassination conspiracy itself, thus gaining information for future blackmail.

In effect, there was a double-down—no, a triple-down—on the Mafia for committing the murder. It was their objective, that of the American conspirators and Castro's as well. With such an array of forces against him, Kennedy had no chance. The Mafia would handle the execution itself, while the domestic conspirators would take care of logistics and cover, and Castro would provide various types of support and additional intelligence. The Cuban Infidel was delighted to participate, considering it worthwhile "insurance". He was not about to take any chances with an enemy like Kennedy, bent on his destruction.

As previously indicated, the Infidel Castro had, in fact, threatened top American leaders with **death** by unequivocally stating that, if they were attempting to get him killed, they themselves would be targets. That, no doubt, was probably dismissed as bluster by the U.S. executive branch, since they brushed it aside and took no effective countermeasures. Some precautions were considered, mainly in lip-service but, in effect, not implemented. No doubt the conspirators, acting from within he scenes and behind them, intervened to dismiss, disguise or ignore any and all warning signs. It was in their own best interests to make sure that any action to enhance the president's protective network be reduced or neutralized.

Since Castro, as an accomplice in the plot, got to know all the details as co-conspirator, he obtained foolproof protection from action by the United States to depose him: any such effort would trigger **revealing the truth about the Kennedy assassination!** No American leader was even willing to contemplate such an eventuality. Result: Castro has since been, in reality, off limits to any serious action against him by the U.S., or even by third countries at all traceable or linked to America. Concealing the truth about the presidential assassination, which benefitted those who then came to power and to some extent still benefits the governmental structure, was and remains far more important than overthrowing a dictator who does not appear to threaten America and is thought incapable of causing any major trouble.

By the way, when JFK was killed, Castro put on an Oscar-worthy show of consternation and praised the dead president to the high heavens. An attitude **precisely contrary** to his previous posture. Precisely aware of the timing, he had even made arrangements to be notified of the event when having lunch with French journalist Jean David, who reported Castro's well-rehearsed reaction on hearing of it. According to David, Castro said these exact words: "That is very bad news."

If you believe that, I have a bridge in Brooklyn I'd like to sell you. Allow me to say that *that* is the most unlikely reaction possible from a man on hearing that his worst enemy has just been killed. He should, of course, have been jumping for joy—and most likely did. But, guess what, he told Jean David what to report! Never mind that he most likely said: "*Al fin, coño!*" (Finally, damn it!)

There lies the fundamental reason for the survival of the Castro tyranny and its consequences throughout the Americas—and for the United States itself—for over half a century.

EPILOGUE. The re-establishment of diplomatic relations with Cuba in 2015 only consolidates the Castro regime, giving it the international recognition it has not needed but still welcomes. The Castro mob has received everything it demanded, perhaps even monetary or other compensation for trumped-up damages, while giving in return not one iota of anything, even symbolically. For example, not a single political prisoner has been released nor has the regime restored any freedoms or human rights whatsoever. Just the opposite! In fact, it has not even made any promises—even if to be later ignored—about the future observance of any niceties regarding such basic concerns.

The Castro mobsters will soon file a claim for billions against the U.S., when the opposite is what should happen, since the Castros "expropriated", i.e., **stole**, billions in U.S. property, never providing a single cent in compensation. Yet we shall soon see American corporations invest billions in the island, oblivious to the risk that, someday, their capital contributions to the Castro family's prosperity will again be taken over, lock, stock and barrel.

And let no one be surprised if, after closing the U.S. extraterritorial prison facility at Guantanamo Bay, the current administration decides to turn it over to the Castro brothers, à la Panama with Jimmy Carter.

In early 2016, the U.S. President Obama fulfilled one of his dreams: he went to Cuba. But he was received not by the chief executive, Raúl Castro—as required by protocol—but by a lowly bureaucrat. After that slight, he was allowed to speak over radio and TV, but only after the Castros had reviewed his text to make sure that he there was nothing they might disagree with.

* * * * *

Back to the conspiracy. The mob, in charge of the actual execution, proceeded to study sites and set-ups. The CIA, the FBI and the Secret

Service would provide all the support and security required. In general, they would be the accessories and conduct things in such a way as to facilitate the hit. Questionable instructions such as removing the top from the presidential limousine, thus clearing the way for the bullets, would be couched in terms of "the President's instructions" and "the President wants it that way". Sharpshooters would be brought in from abroad: it is a rule in this type of action not to use local hit men. It is far better to import the executioners, place them in a safe house until the time of the attack and then slip them out of the country after the deed is done and things cool down. That is precisely what they did.

At least three professionals were smuggled in separately from Marseilles and lodged in a carefully selected safehouse. They only left their premises to scout locations, gather on-the-ground intelligence and further prepare themselves. They perfected a simultaneous cross-firing system to make sure they would not fail and leave a wounded-but-live president in office. The ballistic explosion that destroyed JFK's head was likely the result of two dum-dum (hollowed-out) bullets simultaneously hitting their target.

The autopsy at Bethesda Naval Hospital was carefully rigged: Secret Service and CIA agents were posted to watch and tell the doctors what they were supposed to find. Later, the conspirators got insurance by seeing to it that the President's brain, preserved in a jar of liquid, disappeared from its storage place in the National Archives building. If analyzed—it somehow never was—the brain could have provided evidence contradicting the Warren Commission's single-bullet theory.

Meanwhile, a CIA team was handling the chosen scapegoat, its under-cover contract agent Lee Harvey Oswald, in order to properly frame him. He was told that his mission was to infiltrate a group of anti-Kennedy conspirators and report what he learned. That way, he would be involved, tracked, and be at the appropriate place and time when the hit took place. To further implicate him, he was instructed to order by mail a cheap Italian rifle of World War II vintage, a Manlicher-Carcano, by any standard unsuitable for anything but target shooting (its telescopic sight was an inaccurate add-on). Furthermore, he was told to store it at the building where he worked and also to fire a stray shot or two—aimed away from the President—on the pretext that it would prove the need for bolstering presidential security.

Oswald was used to following instructions and being only partially informed about a given mission: he was familiar with the need-to-know rule. Therefore, he was easily led into the frame-up. Contrary to the story given out by the media, he spoke fluent Russian as an experienced operator who had worked for the FBI, the CIA and military intelligence. He had gone to the Soviet Union as part of a special assignment in which he pretended to be an American defector; to prove his bona fides he tore up his passport and expressed his desire to remain there. Once his assignment was over he was instructed to make known his "disappointment" at life under communism and return, whereupon he went to the U.S. consulate and asked for a new passport. Not only did they promptly comply, but they also gave him some cash for the trip. Further, he brought back his Russian bride, Marina—the daughter of a KGB general! He likely got away with that by agreeing to be an under-cover Soviet agent within the U.S.

Oswald no doubt informed his American intelligence handlers, who approved the arrangement in order to facilitate his exit from the Soviet Union. That way the Soviets, believing he would be working for them, would not stand in his way. At such a point, for all practical purposes, he was a double agent who might have been loyal to either side, or both, according to his own inclinations. But there is no evidence whatsoever that he ever actually spied for the Soviet Union. He was, instead, a useful U.S. intelligence asset who later came in handy as a scapegoat.

Ever since the assassination, all of this has been meticulously covered up. To get an idea of the vast extent of what has been held back, *just* consider this: **not a single note, document, recording or piece of evidence is available about a word said by Oswald during the 48 hours that he was in custody in Dallas**. What? No one asked him a single, solitary question?

Yet there is even more. There appears to have been no inquiry as to his actual cause of death, after he was practically held up as a target for Jack Ruby to shoot. This raises a question: could it be that the surgeons were instructed **not to save him**, but to make sure that he did NOT survive? (Not the first time, or the last, that a scapegoat's death was ensured by medicine.) Was an autopsy performed, as should have been according to standard procedure? If so, was it rigged (like JFK's own)?

We can be absolutely sure that the answer to all of the above is a resounding YES!

But the above is a minor part of the evidence destroyed, ignored, wiped clean or deliberately overlooked. Another curious instance overlooked by the press is that the limousine carrying the President when the fatal shots impacted was immediately shipped back to Washington by the Secret Service and completely overhauled, wiping out all evidence such as bullet holes, blood stains and other significant details that would have determined the number of shots and their direction. For example, the blood spatters and brain particles on the limousine's trunk lid and a motorcycle policeman's windscreen clearly proved that the fatal shot came from ahead.

But the media were not concerned about such details. They concentrated on the tragedy, the family, the sorrow. Investigative journalism practically disappeared as newspapers parroted what was touted as the "official" story: Oswald, acting alone, was the sole perpetrator and not a single trace was found that he had any associates, confidants or assistance whatsoever. By the way, this conclusion was reached by FBI Chief Hoover within hours of the event—can one imagine ANY crime, let alone this magnicide, so open-and-shut as to be immediately "solved" and preclude anything but the most cursory investigation? Hoover sent verbal, never-written instructions that the Bureau's agents NOT come up with a single iota of evidence to the contrary, on pain of dismissal or banishment to Alaska (his favorite destination for disobeying his edicts).

In the meantime, Johnson was busy appointing a hand-picked group of reliable confidants collectively designated as the "Warren Commission". Hoover, as co-conspirator, was against the idea as dangerous, but was overruled by Johnson, who recognized the importance of an unimpeachable body to come up with a final report and thus quiet down any doubters. The task entrusted to the commissioners was supposedly to find out what really happened. Actually, **the objective was to cover everything up**: they got their instructions from LBJ himself, who told them in advance what they had to conclude— that Oswald alone had done the deed, with no accomplices or associates whatsoever. To those commissioners who objected he shook his finger and asserted that it was a matter of national security and anything else might prove to be extremely dangerous, likely to even result in nuclear war. With the Commission's seal of approval, the case was closed and he washed his hands of the whole affair.

One of its members, Louisiana Senator Hale Boggs, dissented from the Commission's single-bullet theory. Later on, as Senate majority leader, he suspected that there was more to the JFK assassination than was at first apparent and announced that he would establish a special senatorial committee to conduct a new, independent inquiry. He also had serious differences with FBI Director J. Edgar Hoover and severely attacked him and his Bureau on the floor of the U.S. Senate.   But before he could launch his inquiry, he mysteriously disappeared on a flight in Alaska together with his top aide, plus Representative Nick Begich, who was facing a tight re-election race in that state. The small twin-engine aircraft, a Cessna 310, vanished and, to this day, some 45 year later, no remains have **ever been found!** There are solid grounds for suspicion that his death was related to his planned inquiry into the JFK assassination. It is worth noting that only by having a powerful bomb explode in flight, tearing the plane to shreds, can such an aircraft's remains be impossible to find from the air.   The alternative is rigging a timing device to the fuel line so it will cut off over the sea, while another one cuts off radio communications. Since the 600-mile flightline from Juneau to Anchorage would run partly over water along the Alaskan coastline, it offered opportunities for sabotage. Bearing in mind that if a pilot runs out of fuel in such circumstances he will most likely attempt to glide to the coast and find a beach suitable for an emergency landing, it is likely that the aircraft was also fitted with a time bomb as "insurance". At any rate, the culprits must have done a perfect sabotage job and, in addition, managed an elaborate coverup, since a 39-day search by Air Force, Navy and Coast Guard planes could find no traces. FBI Chief Hoover and Boggs' other enemies dutifully expressed condolences to his family, no doubt inwardly smiling about having gotten away with it.   In view of the dangerous situation—re-opening the Kennedy assassination inquiry was out of the question for the conspirators—any analysis of the case makes it extremely difficult to accept any "explanation" involving an accident. Nor belief in an extensive "search" that found no traces of the aircraft. Ergo, foul play was involved.   Did   the   media   or   the government itself ever hint at that possibility? Dear reader, make up your own mind.

* * * * *

We are not forgetting about Jesse Rosen, the Mafia operator who consorted with the Dallas police, providing them with free drinks, amateur, free-lance and professional prostitutes, plus rollicking entertainment at his strip joint. In return, they did him favors. A very significant one was making it possible for him to enter the area where Oswald was to be brought out for transfer, so he could have an opportunity to shoot him. He did his job—as well he needed to, knowing the Mafia rule that a bungled job of any importance means curtains, likely preceded by torture and followed by "special care" for surviving relatives. But seeing himself jailed and forgotten, isolated and shunned by his former friends and associates, he gave signs of willingness to talk and told the commissioners that he would, but only if they took him to Washington. Believe it or not, the Commission's response was a threat: "In that case, you'd better not say anything!"

Later, when convicted and sentenced, the government made sure that he would be unable to make waves. Just when his tongue might again have been getting a little loose, they introduced intense radiation into his cell—a tool commonly used by authorities to get rid of trouble-makers. In a short time—guess what—he was found to be suffering from incurable cancer.

Case closed.

CHAPTER III

The Coverup of the Kennedy Murders—
by the Kennedys Themselves

If the fact that John, the President of the United States, was murdered by a conspiracy of top government officials, were not shocking enough, I have news for you:

    a. Once done, the assassination was subjected to a TOP-SECRET COVERUP on the part of the Kennedy family itself, led by the heir to the dynasty, Robert Kennedy—the Mafia's veritable nemesis—who wanted it that way.

    b. The second Kennedy assassination—that of Robert himself—the result of yet another conspiracy born of the JFK elimination, was likewise subjected to a TOP-SECRET COVERUP conducted by the Kennedy family under the leadership of Teddy, the young senator and next surviving heir.

    c. The murder of John, Jr. (nicknamed John-John), president-to-be if he so chose, was a third TOP-SECRET COVERUP, again led by Teddy and maintained, after his death, by the rest of the Kennedys.

Why would the powerful and potentially dangerous Kennedy family, who had had little qualms about "taking care", one way or the other, of people who stood in their way[4], stand still for the murder of not just one of their own, but of their top man, the President of the United States?, no less. Not likely, you say? Well, they had excellent reasons: for instance, protecting the myth that John was a good, honest fellow who came out of nowhere to defeat a tough-guy sitting vice president and pull out a no-holds-barred election by a hair's-breadth, but fair and square. He would not do any back-alley deals to steal an electoral victory, would he?

Well, I have still more news. As we learned from the previous chapter, there was a deal-to-steal in the 1959 election. The Mafia was to arrange for Kennedy to "win"—and so they delivered—and the new administration was to "lay off"—which, to their regret, they clearly didn't. So the Kennedys were in a bind as to bringing to light the truth about the assassination. If they rejected the Oswald hoax and openly pursued the

---

4 See Chapter IV, Marilyn Monroe's "Suicide".

real criminals, the deal-to-steal would come out in the open. That would have been far too messy. They therefore had to support the coverup, pretend to accept the obvious hoax and bide their time. It was a long-term gamble: they would have to play it coy and cool and, once at the top again, see how they could settle accounts.

It was Robert's turn to seek the presidency, and so he did following the usual system. First, become senator from New York, which anyone with his Democratic-party history and pedigree could easily do, and then proceed with his run for the top job. Once there, he would deal with the perpetrators of the deed and even the score. There is no question that he must have been aware of the risk: the Mafia boys would suspect what he was planning and at some point "take care" of him. But he was going to run that risk; he could not possibly let them get away with what they had done and go scot-free.

How he could have possibly reached such a shaky conclusion is a mystery and will likely remain so forever. We can only assume that he was obsessed with the mission of getting revenge and bringing back the days of "Camelot" that his beloved brother so ardently but futilely sought. (The dream called "Camelot" was an illusion, a hoped-for ideal that remained so: it was primarily a creation of the press that so intensely believed in, nay, worshipped him.)

Robert also had a "devil-may-care" streak that pushed him to take chances, go the extra mile, demonstrate his balls and bravado; he would show them that being small in size—a disadvantage against his bigger brothers while growing up—did not in the least deter him from putting others in their place, whoever they happened to be: he was not to be denied. Physical violence had not been beyond his sphere when called for: indeed, rumor had it that he was quite capable of going that far. Intellectually, he was barely average, but he would make up for it in determination—a fairly common compensatory mechanism that has actually taken many beyond their level of incompetence, but made more impactful in his case thanks to his family's name and power.

There was no doubt in his mind as to who was responsible for his brother's assassination. After all, there was the private investigation that was done on his instructions and that, to this day, has remained private and unknown to the public at large. Not an inkling as to the results of that investigation has ever come out: had it revealed nothing new, i.e., that it was actually Oswald and he alone, nothing would have been lost by making it public. That yields a fundamental conclusion: it must have been at odds with the official "fairy tale". Although he knew what happened and who was behind it at the intellectual and pragmatic levels, he wanted confirmation in full detail. But he was careful to keep it all to himself; in fact, the very investigation itself was never so much as mentioned in his lifetime.

Also noteworthy is that he never had anything to do with the Warren Commission. Why not? Why was the dead President's brother ignored by such a body? And why did he ignore *it*. Never did Robert, Attorney General at the time!,[5] offer to testify or provide information, nor was he asked to appear or send any documentation or communication. Further, did he ever comment on the Commission's action to find out the truth, nor on its conclusions? All of this is extremely suspicious, not to say outrageous; yet did the press ever ask him any questions even approaching such a topic? (They quite clearly shied away from it; there is no record that they even made the slightest hint about it.)

In retrospect, it might not be too far-fetched to think that Robert might have had a death-wish. Feeling responsible for his brother's assassination, he might have told himself that it was up to him to make things right or else pay the ultimate price for failure.

That he was on a one-way mission to achieve a particular objective was made clear, perhaps, when he never questioned the also-suspicious murder of Martin Luther King. Even though he tried to placate the black unrest that erupted following the event, he never put two-and-two together—or if he did, he chose to ignore it in pursuit of his own goal. Perhaps getting involved in exploring another great, suspect murder, might have distracted him from his objective and/or brought up questions as to why he had never questioned the murder of his brother. It might have been too close to home. That's the best light one could throw on his neglectful attitude, which was actually neglectful of his duty as a true patriot, public servant and hopeful national leader. It is safe to say that anyone else in his position would have questioned the assassination and called for an independent prosecutor in place of a commission appointed by a likely guilty party.

In any case, we can see that the wounded tiger on the loose was reserving his energy for the final, epic battle against the forces of evil that had taken his brother in the prime of life and derailed the Kennedy Dynasty when it was on the cusp of glory: it was up to him, Robert, to restore it to its proper place.

Having witnessed Robert's attitude and its result, the reaction of the next sibling in line, Teddy, becomes unsurprising. There is, however, a sharp difference: this younger man showed better judgment: he never made an honest-to-goodness run for the presidency. Oh, he pretended to

---

[5] We're following the innovative punctuation standard set in my forthcoming (bilingual) book, *El buen uso impide el abuso / Good Usage Prevents Abusage*. It is a practical matter that question marks, exclamation points, etc., are quite normally inserted in speech within the middle of an utterance. So why shouldn't it be so indicated in writing?, if that is where they belong.

do so, but in a purely symbolic, hopeless effort against a sitting president, Jimmy Carter, who was neither worried about it nor took him too seriously. Carter went through the motions to preserve the nomination for himself, knowing that Teddy was only running a pretend campaign, showing the Kennedy colors for those still enamored of the Camelot dream.

Why Teddy would actually go through all that just for show is an unanswered question best left for future historians. What was the point? To run for the top job with a chance of landing it would have been, in mob parlance, "a ticket to cement shoes"—which is what they certainly had in store for him. So, why the pretense? The rationality of going for something not really wanted is fine if, on stage, one wants to please the crowd, but is not evidence of any intelligence. Rather, lack thereof, one must conclude. In other words, Teddy most surely liked the acclaim and the attention, but the big prize—not on his life! (literally)

* * * * *

This segment, on John F. Kennedy, Jr. (nicknamed Jay-Jay), nearly requires a subchapter. The poor boy had made no public overtures to seek the job. His mother, the sweet, elegant Jennifer, no doubt advised him against it quite early, emphasizing the life-threatening danger that had claimed his father and uncle and still lurked in the shadows of politics. Yet in the back of his mind he dreamed of the presidency and a new edition of Camelot, although confiding such thoughts only to the closest of friends and family.

A couple of days before his death he held a secret meeting in a New York hotel with French intelligence agents who were familiar with the conspiracy that killed his father. In fact, a book was written on the subject in 1968 by an author named James Hepburn (a pseudonym, of course), detailing the hows, whys and wherefores of the assassination. Originally entitled *l'Amerique brule* (America burns), it was published in English as *Farewell America,* but for years was banned within the U.S. and very few copies were smuggled in by individuals. Today it is widely available, though little known.

What John, Jr. confirmed at that meeting was what he had suspected all along, but it moved him to make up his mind to run for president and right the wrongs done to his father and family. French intelligence had penetrated the conspiracy and learned not only the identity of the conspirators but also, after the assassination, about the list of evidentiary materials scheduled to be kept from the public until 2039.

Even at such a late date for entering politics—he was nearly 40— he had the qualities and, most of all, the pedigree—to run for and win the presidency. He was, truly, yet another Kennedy victim in this whole story of greed, power-hunger, glory-seeking and intrigue. John, Jr. was, truly, a decent young man. Like his father, he was gifted with good looks, sociability, and acting skill on stage, in front of any audience. Unlike his father, he was not—although he could have been—a womanizer of epic proportions. His intelligence, perhaps below that of his parentage, was disappointing—he had failed his bar exam several times; however, he did assemble a capable staff to launch a new magazine, "George", with reasonable success. And he had solid instincts and business acumen.

Needless to say, the Mafia kept a wary eye on him. They correctly figured that one day, perhaps soon, the dashing young fellow might make his move and accept the presidency that would most likely be his on a silver platter if he chose to announce his availability. He had by then accumulated experience in a number of areas that would prepare him for the job: publishing, business, high society, some public service, sailing, flying his own aircraft, etc. And, of course, the age requirement (35 years) and sufficient maturity. The top capos worried over that scenario but until then were in no hurry. But now, having no doubt got wind of Junior's meeting with the French intelligence agents and his intentions, they decided the time had come.

They realized the time was ripe for them to nip things in the bud before complications such as heavy security settled in. It would undoubtedly save them a mountain of trouble. And the hit would be simplicity itself: "a lead-pipe cinch", in their lingo. A no-problem job, easily within Mafia capabilities.

The decision carried only minor caveats. It had to be an "accident" leaving no traces, no loose ends, no tell-tale evidence. Oh, it might arouse suspicion, but that would be all. To make matters easier, John's small aircraft was at a small airport in New Jersey and not under any kind of security.

John loved to fly his own airplane, and at some point he would be doing so over ocean waters—the perfect scenario for making him disappear without a trace. When an aircraft goes down over the high seas, no evidence will be recovered of tampering with its fuel line, for example. The engine and nearly everything around it will sink to unfathomable depths.

If a timing device attached to the fuel line cuts off supply in flight, the aircraft will simply go down and disappear beneath the waves. But, there might be time to radio for help or glide to a crash- landing on the nearest beach. In that scenario, survival was possible. Yet it would be unlikely if a small barometric bomb were attached to the tail and detonated via an electronic signal at a certain point during the flight. The explosion, confusion and sudden uncontrolled descent would prevent a distress call. Any evidence of a blast would disappear or be extremely minor.

Although unreported by the press, John, Jr., radioed the airport from 13 miles away that he was coming in for a landing. It was 9:39 p.m. After that, silence. The "spatial disorientation" story does not make sense considering the flight path along a coast lined with lights from multiple cities and towns. It had been his only radio communication during the flight, which means that it took place shortly before the bomb went off. A suitcase belonging to his wife, Carolyn (or to her sister Lauren), was found a number of miles away from the flightpath, meaning that it had likely had been blasted away at the moment of the explosion, whereas the small plane's trajectory took it further away.

John, Jr., his wife Carolyn and her sister Lauren went down forever in the chilly Atlantic not far from their destination, Martha's Vineyard. He was only 38.

Case closed.

CHAPTER IV

Marilyn Monroe's "Suicide"

Poor Marilyn.[6] At one point she convinced herself that President Kennedy, at least in name a practicing Catholic, would divorce his wife Jennifer to marry her. Failing that, she still hoped that she might marry his brother Robert, an even stricter Catholic, who was head of the Justice Department and father to countless children. Never mind that, atop everything, he would be marrying his brother's ex-mistress. But then, she was obviously an intellectually challenged day-dreamer who let her emotions hold sway over her scarce mental talents, far below her sensual physical attributes. To be fair, she had exploited the latter well, thanks to her smarts in ignoring the false, fading socio-sexual mores which nearly everyone paid lip-service to, with a wink while circumventing them. Why shouldn't a girl take advantage of her looks—and brains, she thought. Didn't men?

At any rate she was playing with fire, as Mafia boss and sometime-lover Sam Giancana had told her. "Watch out!", he warned in a rare warm-hearted moment: "sex and politics are an explosive combination." But she wouldn't listen. Instead, she felt ignored and insulted when the Kennedy brothers—first John and then Robert—no longer answered nor returned her calls. She had loved flying incognito to Washington's National Airport, staying at the Mayflower Hotel top-floor suite that John maintained for his paramours, and being escorted through the secret tunnel from Blair House, across Pennsylvania Avenue, to the first family's quarters in the nation's most famous residence. Ah, the trysts with the President were unforgettable; she was enjoying a secret romance with the leader of the free world, and the heady feeling transported her beyond reality. "He said I did wonders for his back", she boasted to her friends, while deluding herself that the top Kennedy would divorce the First Lady and marry her instead. Yet now, all this exhilarating saga was gone by the boards as "Robby"—her pet name for Robert—had also dropped her.

But by now things were completely out of control. She had been diagnosed as **pregnant** and, despite her promiscuity, she was certain that, considering the timing, Robby was the father. *That* was the last straw. Even if he was not, he certainly could be and he ought to be "man enough to own up to it". Yet he had ignored her messages letting him know about such a serious matter.

---

[6] The Marilyn Monroe case is dealt with at length in the author's previous book *Getting Away with Murder—and Costra's Crimes—In U.S. Public Life*. This book provides additional information.

It was time to teach them a lesson, she told a couple of close friends. Publicizing her pregnancy by him and revealing what had gone on with his brother "the Prez", as she called him, sequentially/simultaneously with Robby, would blast their administration to smithereens, while boosting her faltering career into orbit. Just the thought that all her investment in the Kennedys had gone down the drain was beyond painful. Never again would such an opportunity come up. She and Robert had once even gone incognito to a nude beach, disguising only their faces—an escapade they would never forget. It was their private joke, about which they frequently shared a laugh.

But now he had stopped returning her calls. Tough, abrupt, domineering and—as she soon found out—frequently bad-tempered, he could not be crossed. But now she had had enough and her mind was made up. The shattering press conference, to be followed by a tell-all book, would blast them while making her super-popular as a hapless victim of abuse by the rich and powerful. She knew about John Kennedy's numerous other affairs with Nancy Dickerson and other glamorous movie stars as well, and dropping tidbits about that might also be in the offing. It would be just what she needed since her recent falling out with the studio, which had fired her from her starring role in the aptly titled movie "Something's Got to Give". The sensational headlines and feeding frenzy by the press would give her a much-needed boost and restore her slipping career to full-fledged stardom.

It is transparently clear that a woman who is angry at others enough to take these steps is rather unlikely to do herself in. But Robby, who got wind of the situation through brother-in-law Peter Lawford, had other ideas. It was time, he decided, to pay her a visit. His brother, "the Prez", had told him in no uncertain terms that they, the Kennedy dynasty, could take no chances. He had agreed.

As a first step, he called her. She was so weak and willing to believe his every word that she immediately caved. "Sure, sweetheart!, come on over if you can sneak away", she said in her most alluring tones. He said he was busy with urgent Department of Justice work in Los Angeles, but he would make time to stop by, see her and try to patch things up. She was thrilled; maybe they could resume their torrid love affair and, who knew? Oh, he was still fond of her, all right. Mainly of her curvaceous body and skills in bed, hardly of her naïve and mostly empty upstairs.

In their banter over drinks, followed by a session of sex that, as usual, seemed to last longer than clock minutes, she did not broach the subject. Then, in the soft after-glow pillow-talk, she felt the time was right to bring it up, explaining her serious concern over it. Pretending to be shocked—although he knew about it from his brother-in-law Peter

Lawford—he first tried to argue that it would be a disaster for him as well as for her.

"But, darling, what are we going to do?" She used the *we* to make it clear that the problem affected the two of them.

"It would be far preferable to end your pregnancy if at all possible", he argued. If this becomes public, your career would be shot."

"Yes, but I've always wanted a child." He did not miss her determined look.

"Well, if you insist, we'd have to make some fast arrangements." He decided to allay her fears—otherwise his plan would not work. "I'll acknowledge it and do the right thing. "If it comes to that I'll just have to divorce my wife and marry you."

"Oh, sweetheart!" She was overwhelmed on hearing the words she had hoped for, even though she could hardly believe them.

"Rest assured. I'll call you later", he offered, kissing her, as he gathered his things and headed off.

The set-up was in place, he thought. This early visit ensured her being at home for the rest of the evening, when his agents would pay her a final, definitive visit. He would promptly radio his team the go-ahead from his helicopter. Too bad for Marilyn, he told himself, but better safe than sorry.

It was in the Kennedy tradition to get rid of troublesome women. His dad Joseph P. had set the example more than once, most memorably with the girl that he used in order to set up Ari Carthages, the Greek owner of a major chain of motion-picture houses in Los Angeles. Carthages had refused Jonathan's offer to buy him out, and would now live to regret it. The girl framed him in a scandalous under-age rape accusation and subsequent trial that ruined him, and Joseph was able to buy the chain for a fraction of its price. The girl, who was paid money stolen from her by her boyfriend, shortly repented and was about to spill the beans. But all of a sudden she died, apparently from poisoning—yet there was no investigation nor any consequences. Her lips were effectively sealed forever.

Robert was merely following established procedure when he "took care" of Marilyn. She was found in an unusual position—practically straight on the bed, instead of, as in most overdose cases, twisted and contorted. Also she was in a state of undress, i.e., completely naked, which is not how she usually slept. There was no sign of forced entry, no trace of any visitors whatsoever, and the phone not put away for the night as she regularly did before retiring. In short, suspicious circumstances. If, as she often did, Marilyn had taken a sleeping pill, she and her housekeeper would have made the usual arrangements before retiring. If she had gone to the extreme of deciding to take an overdose—

a theory very far-fetched—there might have been indications, such as a note, words with her housekeeper about, say, not wanting to be disturbed for any reason, or other details that someone in such a desperate state of mind might have wittingly or unwittingly revealed.

But no, nothing indicated that anything like that might have been on her mind.

The follow-up was a tragi-comedy, full of slip-ups, bungling and careless mistakes. Her psychiatrist came over when her housekeeper, worried about Marilyn's locked door, called him. Yet she could have done some checking on her own, since she had access to Marilyn's room through a shared bath. The psychiatrist came over, likely found her dead, but chose to not report it until several hours later. Which leads to the conclusion that someone must have threatened him with consequences it he called for help and saved her life; the housekeeper must have been likewise instructed. In other words, the killers wanted to make sure that the drugs in her body had plenty of time to do their deadly work.

It appears that Marilyn was maneuvered into getting a lethal dose of barbiturates through her rectum, thus leaving no traces such as injection marks. This is further confirmed because there were no remnants of capsules or the drugs in her stomach. Besides, if she had purposely ingested a large number of such pills she might have been forced to throw up, or else she might have changed her mind and called for help. Dosage through the rectum, by eliminating the possibility of vomit, is a death sentence.

In short, those behind the deed provided Marilyn's housekeeper with a six-month vacation out of the country and quite likely a lifetime pension. So she was conveniently unavailable until the storm had passed. There was also the unusual behavior of the ambulance team, who gave differing testimony as to the events and their timeline. The investigation was cursory, designed more as show than as an actual inquiry.

After the job was done, there was a scramble to cover it all up, carefully controlled by powerful figures. Besides, neither America nor the world wanted to believe that it could be anything but what the authorities said it was: she did it to herself. Why, even the coroner, the ethnic-Japanese who would coincidentally also autopsy Robert's body six years later, found no evidence to the contrary. Or so he said. The autopsy was inconclusive, ending with the words "probable suicide" —leaving it open to question.

In actual fact, all incriminating evidence was wiped out, removed, destroyed or made to disappear. Her diary, incriminating photographs and engraved items were never found. Why not? Why would she bother to dispose of them? It was a mysterious case, all the authorities admitted, but still refused to thoroughly investigate it. They were backed up by a servile press in the Kennedys' pocket. And the telephone company never released the record of Marilyn's phone calls. Why not, if it tended to confirm that there was no foul play? Is it possible that the telephone record might have been evidence to the contrary? Why, even the Los Angeles chief of police was unusually cooperative—but only to the Kennedys and their agents. He carefully obstructed any objective handling of the case and made sure to support the "official story" of suicide.

Oh, by the way, the chief, a close friend of Robert Kennedy, was promised a major national law-enforcement job if all went well. The Kennedys, it was intimated, were looking to replace J. Edgar Hoover as head of the FBI. Is it possible that such a potential reward might have influenced his behavior? Perhaps. We do know, however, that some time later on the whole file on Marilyn's case disappeared from the L.A. police archives. How strange! When his wife asked him how the investigation was going, the chief answered by drawing a question mark in the air with his finger.

Everyone was sad on hearing the news, but few were suspicious. Hollywood dutifully mourned her. Particularly Joe DiMaggio, who acted as next of kin and handled the funeral arrangements. Heart-broken and angry—he knew about her connection with the Kennedys—he stated in no uncertain terms that no one from that family would be welcome. Yet his suspicions did not come to the point of making comments dangerous to his health. If the movie moguls had *their* suspicions they kept their mouths shut. They themselves had gotten their share of pests out of the way; people who live in glass houses don't throw stones[7]. Besides, Marilyn's career was going downhill. Not their problem.

None of her biographers have indicated that Marilyn had any intention of taking her life. Quite the contrary. She had made some plans for that very same weekend and was hopeful about rekindling her movie career. Peter Lawford, a Kennedy relative by marriage and confidant of his brothers-in-law—who had arranged for Marilyn and the "Prez" to meet at his Malibu beach house on numerous occasions—said that she had phoned him several times that evening to chat and discuss "some concerns". However, for him nothing foreshadowed such an event. At least not that he could recall. If he had had an inkling he would have rushed over to see her, he insisted. But he contradicted himself in different versions, at varying times. Knowing what we now know, Marilyn must have realized something was up and was asking for his help. But she was talking to the enemy: his loyalty was to the Kennedys.

---

[7] One such case was that of William Randolph Hearst, who during a cruise on his private yacht, in a fit of jealousy, killed a man suspected of going after his paramour, movie actress Marion Davies. Never investigated, the case was treated as a suicide. End of story. About the event, Peter Bogdanvich made an excellent movie curiously entitled "The Cat's Meow".

And, as is likely, if he knew something was up he was not about to betray *them* by helping her out.

No biographers were bold enough to come out and say the obvious: that she was likely killed in order to shut her up. No doubt saying so might then have been too dangerous. But, looking at the whole circumstances objectively, no other conclusion can be reached. Those at the top have always found ways of disposing of trouble-makers via accidents, suicides, and induced ailments. And those who dared to make their suspicions public have suffered untold consequences. Accidents, mysterious but untraceable events. Who was going to take that chance?

To be completely fair, it is possible that Marilyn became emotionally despondent on being told directly by Robby, when he helicoptered over to visit her that afternoon, hours before her death, and told her that their affair was over. *That* might have pushed her over the edge and prompted her to take an overdose. Yet that is unlikely considering that, as the most desirable woman on earth, still youthful and powerfully attractive, she could and did choose from among the most famous and powerful men in America.

Nonetheless, one of her last phone conversations that afternoon was with José Bolaños, her sometime Mexican lover. He reported that Marilyn had told him "something shocking", but refused to say what it was. Could it have been her discovery that she was pregnant by Robby?

Reactions to Her Death

When Joseph P. Kennedy, the Clan Patriarch, was informed by his niece about the event, you could have heard a pin drop. He and everyone else within earshot became strangely silent.

Robert Kennedy spent the morning at the estate of his host in San Francisco riding horses and playing touch football as if nothing at all had happened. Later, when Marilyn's death came up in conversation, he is reported to have taken it very lightly, discussing it "in an amusing way", according to a witness.

A famous movie star who starred in "Bonnie and Clyde" and had been a frequent guest at Peter Lawford's beach house and knew Marilyn well, responded with a "no comment" when asked about her death. That has to be the strangest reaction of all: "no comment" on hearing about the sudden death of a youthful actress that he was well acquainted with?!

When Peter Lawford was asked by his last wife (not the Kennedy sister) about Marilyn's death, he answered out of the blue: "She took her last big enema". Precisely. According to the toxicology report no remains of barbiturate capsules were found in her stomach, which brings up the likelihood that she was given a lethal dose via the rectum.

Oh, did I mention that according to the L. A. Police the entire file on Marilyn's death had completely disappeared when about to be looked into a few years later?

CHAPTER V

Chappaquidick: Accident or Crime?

What happened in that peaceful island off Anna's Vineyard on the coast of New England is a question long-dismissed by the authorities, the press and history as a mysterious, unfortunate accident.

An astounding conclusion reached with amazing promptness, considering that someone died, while the survivor showed no visible physical consequences of an accident in which the driver's car fell off a bridge. Supposedly at the wheel was Teddy Kennedy, a senator from a distinguished American "royal" family. Mr. Kennedy, in fact, appeared early the following day in his motel lobby, hale, hearty and chatting with other guests as though nothing at all had happened.

In contrast, he later claimed that immediately after the event he had 1) first attempted to rescue his companion from the car, and 2) then become disoriented, not fully realizing what had happened until morning.

But, did he? Clearly not, since he strolled into the lobby of his hotel, nattily dressed and showing not a care in the world, and chatted amiably with the guests. Was he trying to establish that he had had nothing to do with the accident and, in fact, ignorant of it? Was that performance based on the hope that someone else would take the blame, relieving him of all responsibility?

In fact, *that* had been the tenor of the conversation he had held the previous night, at the scene of the "accident", with George Grogan, his friend since childhood, who had always been his "fixer-upper" whenever there was a problem. Grogan, now an attorney, had urged him to report the event forthwith as the only sensible and viable option. Anything else would be not only dishonest but risking trouble with the law, since there were many after-the-fact witnesses who were aware of what had transpired and had heard his own statement that he was driving. For Mr. Kennedy to deny his role in the event, Grogan argued, would involve a web of lies so incredibly complex that it could not possibly stand up and might, instead, bring up charges of lying under oath and obstruction of justice. Mr. Kennedy ended the discussion by saying that he would "take care of it" and asking Grogan to go back to the cottage and look after the girls who had been invited to the party; then he suddenly jumped into the channel and began swimming across to Edgeville, on Anna's Vineyard. Grogan and his companions were astonished at the turn of events, but took that to mean that Kennedy would report the event without further delay.

Just prior to that exchange, Mr. Kennedy had returned soaking wet to the house where the party was taking place and, once there, had asked Grogan and another guest to come outside and talk in private, inside a parked car. Appearing distraught, he told them briefly about the "accident" and the fact that "Molly Jane was still in the car". That shocked Grogan into taking charge and saying that they had to go back and attempt to rescue Molly Jane, hoping that she might somehow have escaped drowning. Accordingly, they drove back to the scene and attempted to get into the half-submerged car, struggling against the current in the dark of night. After a few minutes they realized that it was no use and gave up. It was at this point that the above-described conversation took place between Kennedy and Grogan.

Notwithstanding the dire circumstances and the fact that a life might have been lost, no one reported the event, not even Grogan; they all kept the news to themselves, perhaps not even telling the other party-goers. Why not? To this day, no one knows because, as we shall see, everyone suddenly vanished from the scene and became unavailable for questioning.

In the meantime, Mr. Kennedy had got back to his hotel and found his way to his room without attracting attention. (Later he claimed that he had been dazed and simply gone to sleep—an incredible piece of *sang-froid* considering what had just happened.) He did, however, wake up the manager at about 2:00 a.m. to ask what time it was. Why would that matter?, you may ask. It has been said in writing—a comprehensive book was written on the subject—that he might have been trying to establish an alibi in case one of his subordinates at the party could be persuaded to say that *he* had been the driver, and not Mr. Kennedy.

Believing that such a story recounts the straight facts takes a stretch of the imagination, or enormously elastic credulity. But let us simply look at the facts. Forty-some years later, an objective review of the event and all surrounding circumstances shows that something was clearly amiss. Actually, **a lot** of things simply do not add up, no matter how one analyzes them; the more one ponders the circumstances the less credible they seem. If it were a jig-saw puzzle, the pieces would in no way fit together.

But in the interest of impartiality, let us review a few of the items on a long list of inconsistencies, false statements and suspicious circumstances.

1. The girl, riding as a passenger in a car presumably driven by Mr. Kennedy, is found dead in shallow water while he, to all outward appearances, seems unharmed when he walks into a police station to report it, **ten hours** after the event.

2. The scene of the presumed accident was not at all unfamiliar to Mr. Kennedy, who asks everyone to believe that he got lost and made a wrong turn.

3. If so, there were no signs of braking before the car went off the side of the bridge and into the water, as one would assume if the driver were paying any attention at all. The bridge goes off at an angle from the road, but the car was not steered to stay on it. Also, only an unreasonable speed would explain where it landed, upside down and facing backwards.

4. Mr. Kennedy provides no information about any conversation with the victim during the episode, nor is there any credible purpose for the drive at that time of night and in so desolate an area. (The speculation that Mr. Kennedy and his passenger were attempting to board the final ferry, at 12:00 midnight, from Tappahannock to the mainland, doesn't hold up: it was too late for it; furthermore, if that was their plan, why did they leave without saying goodbye to anyone?)

5. When Mr. Kennedy walks into a small police station to report what happened it is 10 hours later. He asks for pen and paper and time to write down a statement, which he does after asking for privacy in a separate room. Is that standard police procedure for someone who might have caused an accident? It takes him about 45 minutes to write out a few sentences with terse information of the event, but no mention of a party or any such gathering, nor of going back to the scene with Grogan and another guest to attempt a rescue. He refers vaguely to "a

passenger" in the car, but not to the likelihood of death. Then he calmly walks out the back door; the officer does not stop him or even file charges against him. The press, waiting in front of the police station, is outwitted.

6. The usual procedure of, questioning, asking for full identification and placing a charge is simply skipped. The officer does ask for his driver's license; Mr. Kennedy says that he left it at home, but will bring it in (at some unspecified time).

7. Mr. Kennedy makes a call to the girl's parents to report the event, but does not mention that *he* was driving and that he therefore might be responsible for her death.

8. It is later determined that the girl did not drown, but was likely able to breathe in an air bubble in the upside-down car; i.e., she slowly asphyxiated, after lasting for possibly several hours. This means that she could have been saved if only the accident had been reported and someone had come to her rescue.

9. The circumstances and known facts are sufficient to establish a strong likelihood of an intimate relationship between Mr. Kennedy and the victim. In such cases it is customary to conduct an investigation to rule out foul play. Nothing of the kind was done.

10. The girl's body is not autopsied as required by law. Would the procedure have revealed the actual circumstances of death, such as the presence of barbiturates in her body (that might have rendered her sleepy and unable to make her way out of the vehicle in an emergency)? Most important of all, might the autopsy have revealed the possibility of **pregnancy**?

11. Would such evidence have had a bearing on the event, provided a motive for wrongdoing and indicated that there had been a criminal act—perhaps amounting to **first-degree murder**?

12. The girl's body is spirited off to the home of her parents in another state, where it is quickly buried. The parents refuse the autopsy and no further questions are asked.

13. Mr. Kennedy, charged only with leaving the scene of an accident (a smoother wording for what is actually "hit and run"), is only sentenced to a six-moth loss of license, even though there has been a death in the case (and such a penalty is meaningless for someone who is regularly chauffeured).

14. No civil claims of wrongful death are brought by the girl's family; in fact, there is a strong likelihood that Mr. Kennedy made a financial settlement with them. The press does not probe into that.

15. The guests at the party—approximately twelve to fourteen—are not questioned by the authorities and make no statements to them or to the press, neither then nor ever, as far as is known. The guests were whisked away from the scene and promptly made themselves unavailable.

16. The friends, room-mates and co-workers of Molly Jane made no statements; in fact, they were suspiciously reluctant to talk, even about her personality, habits or job.

17. The case goes to trial based on the minimum possible charge, disregarding the death involved. Afterward, Mr. Kennedy makes a televised statement to the nation, posing not the question of his criminal or even civil responsibility, but simply asking viewers to consider whether he should continue to represent his state in the U.S. Congress. This is clearly not the issue, but it evades it and ends the matter.

18. The press appears to be uninterested in investigative journalism, but intent, instead, on accepting at face value the statements made by Mr. Kennedy and the minimal action taken by the law-enforcement authorities and judicial system of the state where the event took place—which happens to be Mr. Kennedy's and is represented by him in the U.S. Congress.

Readers may now make up their own minds as to what happened. They can accept the "official" version of events as they were recorded at the time, or else consider another, completely different possibility: one that was never even suggested at the time.

Postcript.

When I personally met Leo Damore, the author of the definitive book on Chappaquidick, *Senatorial Privilege,* I asked him if he thought that perhaps the event might have been something purposeful.

The result was unforgettable. The poor man started shaking in his boots, evidently suspecting that I was a plant trying to see if he would let slip a secret that he had been threatened to stay away from. No wonder the entire book gingerly sidestepped the slightest suggestion that the event might have been nonaccidental.

CHAPTER VI

The Bay of Pigs Double-Cross and its Consequence: the 1962 Missile Crisis

Just about everyone has ignored or misinterpreted this betrayal at the top, which cost the United States an enemy at its doorstep and endless strife, trouble and tyranny throughout Latin America. Its results: a 56-year disaster (and counting) that has brought more harm, more enduringly, to the cause of democracy, freedom and respect for human rights in the Western Hemisphere, Africa and the world than any other event in history. (Hitler's period of rampant insanity lasted less than 20 years.)

No one has ever wanted to say it—out of respect for the memory of this overestimated hero of the ages who was cruelly murdered, thus achieving Lincolnian stature in death—, but it's about time someone did. It was clearly and blatantly a case of cowering under pressure, caving to blackmail. The man, whatever his virtues, was unfortunately weak under threat or serious pressure. Oh, he put on a show of strength and "vigah", but that's all it was: a put-up for purposes of show. Other sharp leaders easily saw through it and took advantage.

Such cleverness was a key ingredient in the personality of the Infidel Castro, a true genius at geopolitics and double-dealing. His invitation to the Soviet Union to come into the island and, by becoming his partner, provide him with unconditional backing against a world power like the United States, was a solid part of the equation, which he exploited to the utmost. But he had all sorts of aces up his sleeve. One of them was, quite likely, photographs and film of the future president, on vacation in Havana during the 1950s, participating in playful encounters with several Cuban mulatto girls—famous for their sexual talent. Then a senator, Kennedy recklessly let his Mafia acquaintances—probably Santo Trafficante and Meyer Lansky, the mob's financial brain, who owned the Riviera Hotel by the seaside in the Vedado suburb of Havana—treat him to these earthly delights. They of course arranged to film the proceedings in case they ever needed leverage from a congressman; foresightedly, they also banked on the chances that so prominent a figure might one day be in the White House—and therefore in their pocket. They merely followed SOP, standard operating procedure.

It's not at all difficult to envision, in hindsight, that such a development was the only possible explanation for the unlikely survival of the Infidel amid earth-shaking events that would have wiped out other gamblers in near and distant world venues. Why, the Bay of Pigs invasion would have been a lead-pipe cinch if the original plan had been implemented: it involved full U.S. air support, with bombing, strafing and calling in the Marines once the beachhead had been established.

But no, the plan was scaled down and doomed to failure by Kennedy's trumping of the Chiefs of Staff every step of the way, to the chagrin of them all as well as of the CIA—which, to boot, was blamed for the defeat! That failure brought on an even worse disaster, the October Missile Crisis, when the Soviets nearly succeeded in installing nuclear missiles 90 miles away from our shores. That should never have come up but for the Bay of Pigs defeat. Even though it was caught just in the nick of time, it was still another major defeat: the USSR maintained its Cuban air, naval and intelligence base, while Kennedy agreed to not invade **nor allow other countries to do so**. More about the pyrrhic Missile Crisis victory in the chapter on that subject.

Kennedy had given other evidence of weakness in the face of daring and blackmail from his enemies. One such instance was his sudden change of heart on nominating his running mate for the presidency. He had already chosen a stalwart senator (from Missouri), Stuart Symington, a man of strict integrity and principles, when Lyndon B. Johnson confronted him at the last minute. Either he accepted him as his vice-presidential candidate or certain revelations were to come out, among them no doubt his sexual adventures. Oh, Lyndon would have nothing directly to do with it, but certain parties would make sure that it became public knowledge if things did not go as expected. This will be discussed in more detail in Chapter VI.

Since Castro had got wind of Kennedy's weaknesses, he knew how to play his cards. JFK's fun and games in Havana would be made public and the world would see evidence and know about his so-far suspect but unconfirmed leanings (at the time, the U.S. public was extremely sensitive about sexual subjects, not to mention consonant racial mixing). Castro might have exaggerated and lied about the evidence he had—we will likely never know what it consisted of, at least during our lifetime.

Very carefully, John made adjustments in the invasion designed to make it fail without giving the appearance of anything but underestimation, mistakes, mishandling, and oversights. He would then blame the disaster on the CIA, a handy scapegoat that he had planned in any case to overhaul so as to make it an instrument of his own that he could more closely control. The irony, of course, was that if the CIA had had its way the invasion would have succeeded; it was only due to the President's undue alterations that it did not, against the advice of the Agency itself and of the Joint Chiefs of Staff.

Neither the commander in charge of the naval task force off the coast of Cuba, nor the Air Force, nor the Marines, nor the Army forces standing at the ready, nor the U.S. naval and military forces stationed in Guantánamo Bay could understand why the President was so reticent. All he had to do was give the order to use the Guantánamo sanctuary to simultaneously launch an offensive from within it that would have wiped out their target's will to resist and brought about total collapse of the Castro government. Every single one of those top military officers expected him to drop the hands-off pretense when the chips were down and order U. S. forces into action. Why, the original plan called for such a move as soon as the invading force was ashore and had established, within hours, a viable beachhead. (As we know, once a deed is consummated, such minor chronometric and other details are brushed aside.)

And yet, as the invasion proceeded and one step led to the next, President Kennedy denied the pleas and outright begging by the top generals to allow any action by the U.S. in support of the freedom fighters. Disconcertingly, the chief executive insisted that the U.S. could not appear to be in any way involved.

"But Mr. President", said the irritated Chief of Staff when he could no longer stand it, "we *are* involved". Recorded history evidences that Kennedy did not directly address that, but instead reasserted that *he* was the one in charge. He did, however, offer one "concession": he directly authorized the carrier-based fighters, already in the air, to conduct "overflights" of the battlefield—but, disconcertingly, without firing a shot. *That*, of course, was the kiss of death, worse than nothing. When Castro's ground forces and his World War II aircraft realized that it was all a toothless move for appearances' sake, they immediately got the message: the U.S. had abandoned its own operation—in a word, given up, doomed it to failure. Their spirits soaring, they felt safe to launch an all-out offensive, unconcerned about any complications such as a Guantánamo-based offensive, landings elsewhere on the island or other unexpected moves. It was over.

Without any such invasion attempt, Castro might have at some point been deposed or subjected to a powerful guerrilla campaign within the island. But the victory at what the Castro-ists call "Playa Girón" gave the Infidel such a boost, an air of invincibility, that he consolidated firm, unshakable control over the island and its people. No one dared oppose him now that he seemed a man of destiny, an unstoppable machine designed to change history and rise to unthinkable heights of power. No one could have possibly imagined that Cuba, 90 miles away from the U.S., could convert to communism and thus become a base of operations for Moscow in the Caribbean.

Immediately, plans took shape to equip Cuba with Soviet troops and, incredibly, nuclear-tipped missiles. Shaken by the Bay of Pigs failure, Kennedy was reluctant to even think about such a development. This was amply demonstrated by the fact that U-2 overflights of Cuba were not—as they should have been—more frequent and intensive, but instead waned, becoming slack and haphazard. U.S. knowledge of the missile emplacements under construction in Cuba and the lack of intelligence thereon—due to Kennedy's own weakening of the CIA—was an encouraging factor, well-noticed by Soviet spymasters. The gremlins in the Kremlin ordered full speed ahead for the missile operation. Before the Americans would know it, the USSR would have a nuclear capability in Cuba able to wipe out Washington, New York and Philadelphia within a 30-minute span.

It was only last-minute luck that brought about photographic evidence of the Soviet missile build-up. After weeks of cancelled overflights—concern about the U-2 shot down over Russia during the Eisenhower administration, would you believe?, dampened the urge to do so over Cuba. In fact, one U-2 and its pilot were lost when shot down by a Russian anti-aircraft missile; it was rumored that the Infidel himself had shoved aside the Soviet gunner, sat down at the controls and pulled the trigger. What did the U.S. do about that?: nothing. Luckily, this deterrent did not actually worsen the President's already weak posture: he took it lying down and made no response. Luckily for us, a lone aircraft had, just prior, happened to take a picture that, enhanced and analyzed, showed incontrovertible evidence of nearly-ready missile-launching sites.

* * * * *

Had the Soviet missiles been ready to fire, the outcome would have been quite different. As it was, the U.S. still lost the battle—despite claims of victory by the administration and its acolytes, the press. Well, yes, the Soviets presumably backed down and ordered their missile-bearing ships to return home. But the provision for on-site inspection was ignored and the administration gave up major trump cards in the process. Firstly, it secretly promised to withdraw U.S. missiles in Turkey—after a reasonable interval enabling it to pretend that this was a one-sided, unlinked initiative for unspecified strategic reasons. Secondly, it promised a) to not invade the Soviet pawn in its back yard, and b) to prevent third parties from attempting any such move. And thirdly, it did nothing to stop, control or remove the presence of Soviet military forces in Cuba. Thus, they could still threaten America at close range, support their pawn at will and expand their influence throughout the region. Which they did, assiduously. The Russians and lately the Chinese have had and still maintain military, intelligence and communications-intercept facilities in Cuba that enable them to pick up a wealth of information and conduct cyber warfare.

In other words, as a result of the Missile Crisis the Soviet Union wound up with a permanent base in Cuba and there was nothing the United States could or would do about it. The Monroe Doctrine torn to shreds. Somehow, the U.S. got extremely lucky that its president, known by his foreign enemies—his domestic ones were another story—for his weakness in facing threats and blackmail, was not thrown completely with his back against the wall.

Still, the U.S. was handed a major strategic defeat that sent it reeling on its heels and would have unsuspected far-reaching consequences.

CHAPTER VII

Exit Hugo Chávez After a Job Well Done

I will start—just because it is a novel question not at all analyzed by anyone else that I know of—with the mysterious death of Chávez in Cuba/Venezuela (when the location of death is in doubt, let alone the date, something's fishy).

The rise to power of this ignorant, stupid military officer was no happenstance. It was a coup carefully planned by a greedy, power-hungry mobster (not a typo, although *monster* is just as perfect a fit), created in the largest Antillean island just to the south of Florida by the son of a Galician migrant—hopeful of making a fortune—whose criminal empire succeeded beyond his father's wildest dreams. Castro senior was a true "operator", as demonstrated by the genes inherited by his first legitimate child, whom I shall generously call "the Infidel".

But let us get back to our subject Hugo Chávez. As we know, he made his name in 1992 by leading a near-successful coup against the democratically elected government of Carlos Andrés Pérez. But most do NOT know who put him up to it. Can you guess? Putting two plus two together, it could have been none other than the Infidel himself, who had long wanted to get his hands on Venezuelan oil to fuel his merciless guerrilla warfare against Central and South American countries as well as his neighboring Caribbean islands (Jamaica, Grenada, Dominican Republic, Puerto Rico, etc.). That strategy would also serve to enhance this demagogue's anti-U.S. stance (anti-Americanism is and has been since the 19th century a populist/popular drug throughout the Hemisphere), and boost his pretense of leadership while shielding him from any U.S. attempt to control him. He surmised that America would be too busy dealing with wildfires in convulsive areas under his attack to deal with the root cause: he, the Infidel himself.

He had extended invitations to potential Latin American leaders that might succumb to his influence and come under his sphere of influence, among them Chávez and his hand-picked successor Maduro, actually anointed and appointed by the Infidel himself. This man was an uneducated truck driver whose lack of intellect was compensated by "socialist" economic instruction received in Havana—of all places. There are now numerous other Cuban satellites: Nicaragua's Ortega, ensconced in practically permanent and total power, Bolivia's hardly literate Evo

Morales, and El Salvador's Sánchez Cerén, formerly a *Comandante* of the Farabundo Martí Popular Liberation Forces, i.e., the Infidel-backed guerrilla movement that shed the country's blood for well over a decade. But Venezuela was a prize worth a major and special effort. Therefore, it is safe to assume that Chávez—as well as Maduro—had personally visited the Infidel, in Cuba, secretly and frequently enough to determine their reliability and come fully under his control.

One need not be a sage to reconstruct the most likely scenario—ignored by the press and pundits for who knows what unspeakable reasons. The Infidel must have trained and indoctrinated Chávez and sent him back with instructions: first, he was to lead the well-planned military coup referred to. If he succeeded, he would seize power in the name of reformers and revolutionaries in order to "wipe out corruption and improve the lives of ordinary Venezuelans". If not, he would become a household name and, after a brief and "unjust" prison term, run for office in the name of the people and true democracy. By the way, he would take no chances and ensure victory at the polls through the usual means: widespread fraud, bribery and threats. Then he would, through intimidation and further electoral "fixes"—let alone brute force, if necessary—make sure of remaining in power indefinitely. The Infidel would provide him with reliable agents and all necessary assistance.

Oh, by the way, this was Adolf Hitler's plan, copied in his bid for power by the Infidel himself, who went dear Adolf one better. Instead of openly invading neighbors, particularly those bigger and more powerful, he would apply slyly adjusted methods to his plan for overseas expansion. Although he preferred armed struggle and bloodshed (like Hitler), he did so by proxy so as to offer plausible deniability, and therefore a degree of immunity. Eventually he became more practical, coldly calculating and non-Hitlerian, realizing that guerrilla warfare was too slow and costly. Half a century of supporting and financing such tactics in Colombia, for example, had not yielded the result he hoped for. In Venezuela itself, in the early 1960s, he had tried to spark a guerrilla movement by shipping in weapons caches and supporting groups that had a chance to seize power through violence, but to no avail. The country was too prosperous for recruiting enough malcontents to sustain an effective guerrilla campaign.

So, starting his long-term planning back in the 1970s, he began implementing his scheme of infiltrating democratic governments with the likes of Chávez and Maduro. Sure enough, Chávez was ambitious and reckless enough to attempt the coup, then spend some time in prison (only two years) and come out as a personality with enough name-recognition to run for president.

Just in case, the Infidel's scheme had Maduro as a back-up. Even more ignorant and stupid than Chávez, Maduro was better indoctrinated, more pliable and reliable. Judging by his public pronouncements and behavior, his formal education was on the order of a grade-school dropout's, and his regular truck-driver job was the only employment he was not disqualified for. No formal academic training, skills, nor desire to acquire them. His careful programming in Cuba made him grateful, obedient and compliant. In short, he was exactly what doctor Infidel ordered for what "ailed" Venezuela, i.e., a brainless puppet whom he would control from a distance in the event that, God forefend, anything happened to Mr. Chávez. That, as we shall see, was not far from the Infidel's visionary machinations. (There is no denying that the Infidel is one of the great political—and evil—geniuses of the 20th century.)

Following the Infidel's Hitler-inspired script, a cretinous Chávez eventually, with the help of numerous on-site, carefully chosen Cuban advisors, climbed to the presidency. Shortly after his inaugural, in 1998, oil-prosperous Venezuela began to go downhill. It is unclear whether that was according to plan—the Infidel had purposely destroyed Cuba's economy for reasons to be explained later in this book—or simply because of Chávez's complete ineptitude and larceny; but it certainly didn't hurt his total control. When people are threatened/bribed/tortured into submission they become wary of sticking out their neck and concentrate on working within the system in order to subsist or simply survive. Open-street killings, if not mysterious deaths, have a powerful persuasive effect.

Hugo's "reelection" in 2006 could not possibly be based on popularity considering the tattered economy, the state of lawlessness, corruption and total mismanagement; yet it was the classic "lead-pipe cinch", since he would under no circumstances allow a free and fair electoral process. Under the guidance of his Cuban "advisors" and a cadre of effective "fixers", he won by a decisive margin of 60%. Officially, that is—the truth being that he lost, most likely taking less than 40% of the vote. (Computers and their handlers are quite capable of reversing actual results—not just in the southern hemisphere but in its northern counterpart as well—a fact carefully ignored by the U.S. media, trained, canine-like, to repress barking.)

But Chávez had one fatal flaw. He began a "Bolivarian Revolution" in Latin America that began spreading to neighboring countries. For his Cuban headmaster that was, well, okay—let us say, acceptable. But he also OVERSHADOWED the Infidel—making him, heretofore the great anti-U.S. Leader of the Hemisphere, upset and uncomfortable. Oblivious to this, Hugo grandstanded as the hero of "XXIst Century Socialism", threw money around to influence politics beyond his borders and—worst of all—did not ship over all the free petroleum that he, the Infidel, thought worthy of himself! In a word, he ruffled the feathers of his master and patron, the very Godfather (yes, a Mafia leader with unbridled political power!) who had enthroned him. But he was too stupid to understand that unforgiveable sin. Why, it was clear as mountain-spring water! Those who might have eclipsed the Dear Leader of Cuba had disappeared from the scene at a steady, unrelenting clip: *Comandante* Camilo Cienfuegos, *Comandante* Huber Matos, *Comandante* Che Guevara, *General* Arnaldo Ochoa (the major Cuban military leader in the Angola proxy war whom people saw as a hopeful national leader A.C., After Castro) and many others. The Infidel's own brother Raúl had also been in the tyrant's sights, miraculously spared only because he was needed and absolutely trusted (the Dear Leader himself so told his brother on a number of occasions: "Raúl, you are so stupid! —if you weren't my brother I would give in to the urge to get rid of you once and for all." The younger half-brother trembled in his boots, scared to death.

Chávez, as the Infidel had correctly envisioned, eventually got too big for *his* boots. No matter, Maduro was waiting in the wings. The Infidel set his trap. But first he was forced to move heaven and earth to rescue Chávez from a coup d'etat that nearly did away with him and his regime. The overthrow failed, it is popularly thought, because of bungling and uncoordinated action by his opponents. The truth, however, is that the Infidel put all his resources into the fray: the personal advisors assigned to Chávez by Castro, and his ample security staff, went full force to the rescue, plus additional forces urgently flown in from Havana, all of which likely saved his life and government. According to the coverup, of course, it was thanks to his popularity that the coup failed.

Once Chávez re-established his control over the country and became stronger than ever, the Infidel's plans began to take shape. He provided him with a special house on a beautiful beach near Havana, where he could have anything he wanted: the best food and drink, wines, movies, women and porn to enjoy them with. When he felt Maduro was ready and the timing was right, the Infidel would make his move. Meanwhile, it was all fun and games for Hugo. He could fly in any time he wanted for mini-vacations, get together with his handler the Infidel and consult on his next moves. He was treated with such warmth and hospitality—as well he should have, considering the fortune in oil he was regularly gifting to his host—that he never suspected anything could be amiss.

That is, until he felt the first pangs of cancer. The affliction began eating up one of his internal organs, probably the liver. The Infidel, smiling inside, pretended shock. How was that possible, Hugo being in good health and only in his mid-50s? "What awful luck!", he commented.

"But it will be all right", he reassured him, "we'll fight it together. I'll be in your corner with all of Cuba's resources."

"I'm thinking of going to Switzerland, where I can get the best medical care and see how soon I can get over this", he said as the Infidel looked pensive and serious, hand on his chin.

"That sounds good, Hugo, but think carefully. You know, about what they can actually do medically, their security, etc. I just want to remind you that we have the best medical care in the world here in Cuba—the most advanced—and we can really protect you, take care of you right here, close to home. You'll have everything you need; not only for you but also for your loved ones who may come to visit any time. We also have "maximum security", the safest place in the world for you **and** them. I will get you the best doctors, the ones who take care of me personally.... Besides, they are actually researching a new cure for your problem. You'll be the first to get it." The Infidel was a practiced, skillful liar—prevarication was an art he enjoyed and had carefully perfected. "We can't let anything defeat someone like you and scuttle our plans to move forward in our mighty, combined struggle."

"That's very kind of you, my friend." The offer was tempting to Chávez. Besides, he would be among friends who spoke the same language. "Let me think about your generous offer." He pretended to be undecided, although his mind was made up: the Infidel's words were invariably irresistible. There was something parapsychological about the way he seemed to read others' thoughts and say precisely the right words.

* * * * * *

The treatment Chávez got, back in his country, seemed at first to be working. But then it did not, so he made arrangements to receive, in Cuba, the special treatment the Infidel had offered him. Besides, if he felt well enough, he could get a good dose of sex while he was there—in Switzerland that would be difficult, at best. Those Nordic, Austro-Germanic, disciplinarians would probably look askance at it and make moves to obstruct any such thing!

Cuban sex being the best in the world, according to rumors, and most certainly in Chávez's own experience, he did get a good dose of it from Cuban *mulatas* who took turns pleasing him individually or two or three at once. At the same time, he was getting a good dose of something else: intense radiation under his bed. That was the "treatment" the Infidel had promised him, and he was delivering it in spades. He had had enough of this clown and was "taking care of him" as promised, hoping to definitively dispose of him as soon as possible. "Why should this clown be stealing my thunder throughout Latin America—and having so much fun, besides!" The Infidel was a jealous, envious taskmaster who particularly enjoyed betraying those who dared rival his high standing, especially if they were unsuspecting friends.

It never crossed Hugo's mind that the Infidel could be capable of such treachery. Not after he had made him the ruler-for-life of Venezuela. Not after, he, Chávez, had given him free petroleum on a regular basis, totaling into the billions of *dólares* a year.

The Infidel, on the other hand, felt Hugo had been a skimpy ingrate in skimpily compensating him for his invaluable services. He would soon teach him an unforgettable lesson and replace him with Maduro, who was already getting on-the-job training running Venezuela in his absence, and with whom he had a much better understanding. Maduro was far more compliant and reliable.

In the later stages of Chávez's radiation-induced sickness, the Infidel's visits to his victim/prisoner in his Cuban mansion gradually became less frequent and finally ceased altogether. Maduro was safely ensconced in power and would control the result of Hugo's last election—in which, as his vice-presidential running mate, Maduro would be the inheritor and real winner. Unsurprisingly, the dying Chávez—without so much as personally campaigning—"easily" won the rigged election while Maduro and the Infidel toasted and tasted an easy "victory" at the polls. (When a candidate with one foot in the grave wins an election in a cake-walk one might suspect something fishy.)

The details, as with everything else regarding the secretive, North-Korea-like regime, are unclear. But it is worth speculating that, toward the end, it *might* have occurred to the greedy Chávez that the most dangerous thing in the world was not being an enemy of the Infidel, but his friend. It was his favorite sport to double-cross his closest associates when they least expected it.

EPILOGUE

At this date—late 2016—Maduro, the truck-driver-turned-puppet-president, is safely entrenched in power as the country crumbles into bankruptcy, rampant corruption and lawlessness. Consumer goods—even toilet paper! —are long-gone from shelves and rationing, a Cuban "tradition" for 50-some years, is taking hold amid a rampant black market. In short, an utter disaster from which Venezuelans, like Cubans 50 years earlier, are fleeing to Florida and other foreign locales.

CHAPTER VIII

Assassination of Martin Luther King

"That communist has to go." FBI Director J. Edgar Hoover's words echoed in the surrounding silence. No one dared contradict him. He stared at his underlings. "Find a way to do it! That's your assignment. He has done enough damage to this country."

His second-in-command, Assistant Director and lover Clutch Towson, nodded in assent and looked at his friend and co-conspirator, General Segretti, head of Army Intelligence. They had worked together before, but this was a major and special job. It would have to be done carefully so as not to provoke the black population to further rioting, pillaging and burning. President Johnson had said there had been enough of that to get civil rights legislation passed and had no appetite for more. Particularly considering his offensive in Viet Nam and the likelihood that the civil rights struggle might combine with the anti-war movement into a violent, explosive package.

So the patsy this time had to be the epicenter of an air-tight case.

Hoover was practically licking his chops. His hatred of blacks had gotten more intense as he had seen them "invade" the city of Washington, taking over whole neighborhoods. Why, during his childhood blacks were few and far between—servants and nannies in his household—as compared to their present numbers. Now, their constant presence and proximity was a reminder of the not insignificant black blood coursing in his own veins, something that a keen observer might notice by facial-feature analysis. Therefore, no side-by-side comparisons for him: blacks in the FBI, such as there were, could hold only menial jobs such as janitors and messengers. At higher levels, the FBI had not a single black employee until he finally hired one to be his driver. He even made the man a special agent so that he could crow that he had a "Negro" in that category, thus keeping Robert Kennedy off his back. At that point Hoover had Robert on his hit list—in fact, his fuse was growing short—and he was anxious to throw him a block of some sort, while he could, and perhaps throw him off balance. He was sure that Robert, the former heir-apparent to the White House, would be dangerous if he learned that anything was planned against King, even though he would still be able to blackmail him just as he had done with his brother, President John F., with his files about their abundant extramarital sex. So the King operation would have to be carefully conducted so as to keep Robert from suspecting anything. And it needed to be done soon, since otherwise Martin Luther King would rise to untold heights.

At the moment, the black movement was getting out of hand. Their civil rights push, sponsored and supported by President Johnson, threatened to make them a powerful political force—precisely what the Commander in Chief intended. But for Hoover the disappearance of King, their top leader, would at least put a damper on their ambitions. Johnson was reluctant to accept Hoover's view, but felt that the deed would not be detrimental to his own agenda of winning the black vote for himself and his party. The killing of King, he knew, would unleash a violent reaction from the black community, but would quell the black upsurge and contribute to his long-term goals.

For his part, Hoover felt that the genie had slipped out of the bottle and it was time to put on the brakes. But Johnson, preferring to give the impression of reluctance, finally gave a secret okay to Hoover, who was extremely insistent. Johnson had not wanted to know anything at all about the operation, but remain at arm's length. Even though he pretended reluctance about the King operation, down deep in his racist past the traditional discriminatory Texas roots were still stirring: in his heart he was as anti-Hispanic as anti-black. Those ethnic groups were, for him, inherently unequal to the basic Anglo-Saxon majority. Yet he kept those feelings hidden by pointing to his great pro-black achievements in civil rights: as he had said more than once, he had put "the black vote in the Democratic party's column for the next two-hundred years". And he had clearly ensured that by legislation paving the way for blacks to register and vote—which they were doing in increasing numbers.

Hoover, finally!, got what he wanted: the okay to go after King. After years of getting nowhere by planting illegal bugs everywhere the civil-rights leader stayed, ate or talked—Martin had taken to holding meetings in hotel lobbies to avoid being recorded by the FBI—, he would take care of him once and for all. That Johnson wanted to know nothing about it was actually better for Hoover. No need to get the President involved in the details—he, Hoover, would tend to those in his own efficient and effective manner. Any Johnsonian "interference"—as Hoover called it—would only complicate matters.

Now, to put the plan into action. Army Intelligence (AI) would take care of the deed itself: his second-in-command at the Bureau, close friend and lover-boy Clutch Towson, had been a high-ranking civilian official at AI, and maintained close contacts with them as accomplice in secret and illegal operations. The only decisions remaining in the King case would refer to place and time—and finding the perfect scapegoat. But Hoover's mind was made up: it had to be done within the next few weeks: neither he nor the country, he felt, could afford a longer wait.

"So, we're down to these three individuals." Hoover's words were a statement, not a question.

"Yes, sir." His assistant and top Bureau official spoke in a firm voice. "As you can see, only one of them has what we consider the ideal qualifications; the other two, only in special circumstances." It sounded like selecting from among job applicants.

"That's quite clear. Your next move is to outline the steps necessary to set it up and ensure it will work properly." His precision-oriented bureaucratic mind had rejected the phrase "set the trap", which is what he had in mind. "We must act swiftly, so get to work on it and get back to me by Monday." It was late Thursday afternoon, so everything had to be done in one to two working days, although in his world the Bureau's work went on 24/7, regardless.

"Yes, sir." The response was, again, firm. No ifs, ands or buts were acceptable to the Director. If something went awry and the assignment had not been completed, there would be hell to pay—even if they came up with a plausible excuse.

Hoover picked up the file and handed it over to his assistant as if to say "take this and run with it—or else".

His assistant received with both hands the original, marked "DO NOT FILE", went to his special safe for such material in an adjoining room and opened it with the combination known only to him and to his virtual domestic partner and hand-picked Assistant Director, Clutch Towson; he put the file in its proper place, shut the door firmly and twirled the dial.

He turned to the group and swept his gaze across it to silently re-emphasize "don't even think about leaking any of this". His message came across loud and clear.

Early the following Monday, Hoover sat before his special group and asked for the report, motioning with his head for his Assistant Director to begin the briefing.

"We are all set, sir. Based on additional research over the weekend," he thus emphasized that they had worked overtime—but not charged for it, in case the Director checked— "the selected candidate, who goes by the name James Earl Ray, is the best we can hope for at the present time. We are in a position to get him to plead guilty using confidential information available to us. We do not expect much difficulty in getting him to see it our way, the consequences for noncompliance being far worse for him. Before proceeding, we will of course approach Ray and make everything crystal clear. The only guarantee we need give him is that we will not seek nor apply the death penalty", the Assistant Director said, coming to the point in a business-like manner, careful to make cursory eye-contact with his friend, superior and life partner, before ending: "We feel certain that this will be incentive enough; otherwise, his fate will be sealed."

"I take it then that this Ray is the best candidate you can come up with." Not particularly pleased, Hoover was equally business-like. The author of the best-selling *Masters of Deceit*—which kept royalties pouring into his personal coffers—could not resist allowing himself a few words of self-serving reassurance that everything was for the public good: "Ahem. Future generations will be grateful to us for this, an essential requirement for the security of our country. With your help, we are ensuring immunity from the danger within: communist infiltration. It's the least we can do."

"There is no question about it, sir." Every one of those present expressed those same words, similar ones, or firmly nodded agreement. They were all middle-aged white men.

They did not tell the FBI Director that a lot of work would still be necessary in order to bring the "candidate" around, mainly through Raul, a shady character involved in lucrative crimes such as narcotics smuggling, who exerted considerable control over Ray and would have to deftly and smoothly maneuver so as to incriminate him in the deed, placing him at strategic locations and compromising circumstances.

The plan called for not letting Rays survive very long after the assassination of King. It called for "clipping" him, Oswald-style, as soon as possible, since putting him on trial would be extremely dangerous, even if he pleaded guilty. A slip of the tongue or a change of heart, and everyone would be in serious trouble. To quickly eliminate him was not only much safer, but clearly essential.

However, a series of mishaps, slip-ups and unforeseen hang-ups arose that threw a monkey wrench into those best-laid plans. Ray, as we shall see, not only survived but would eventually get a new trial and come close to freedom.

Although the deadly shot was likely fired from the Illinois Central Railroad Building, across from the Lorraine Motel, the Memphis Police Department, the FBI and other law enforcers maintained that they came from the bathroom of another building more conducive to implicating Ray. Martin Luther King had had a FEELING that he wouldn't last much longer, and had explicitly said so: "I may not get there with you", he stated in one of his last speeches, the "I have a dream" address at the Lincoln Memorial during the historic Washington civil-rights demonstration.

The marksmen had no doubt staked out the area and carefully prepared for the job they had been assigned. Accomplices had persuaded Ring and his group to stay at the Lorraine Motel—not his preferred lodging in Memphis—and at the last minute even managed to switch him to a room one floor up, with a balcony, where he would be an easy target.

There is so much information indicating that the assassination was a set-up that it would try our readers' patience to explore them all. This was not, by the way, the first time that an attempt on King's life had been planned: his demise had been at the top of Hoover's hit list for several years. But he was hopeful that this time it would work. All the circumstances seemed conducive to success.

Here is a brief, partial list of the curious details.

1. Ray had no motive to commit the deed; there was no racism nor other evidence of bigotry in his past to drive him to such an extreme.

2. Ray was not prone to violence of any kind. He had a record and been imprisoned for only bloodless, relatively minor crimes. The authorities falsely charged him with a bank robbery in order to "enrich" his criminal history.

3. Ray was manipulated in order to provide circumstantial evidence to implicate him. For example, someone drove around in a white Mustang nearly identical to his in order to incriminate him.

4. Ray was maneuvered to place him in the area of the murder, but there was no proof that he was at the precise time and location required for him to have fired the shot.

5. The bullet extracted from King's body was whole, nearly pristine, and never traced to the purported murder weapon. The conspirators at some point replaced it with another, fragmented bullet, that did not allow for such a tracing.

6. The investigation carefully avoided looking into possibilities that someone other than Ray did the deed.

7. Ray was mysteriously persuaded to plead guilty instead of going to trial. They achieved this partly by promising to withhold the death penalty, whether legally applied or otherwise—i.e., "accidentally", "suicidally", via a mysteriously induced illness, poisoning, etc.

8. There were attempts to kill Ray during his imprisonment.

9. Multiple obstructions were thrown into the legal system, law-enforcement investigation and other avenues to concentrate on Ray and convict him.

10. Once imprisoned, the state and federal authorities did everything they could to prevent Ray from appealing, getting a new trial or seeking any form of redress.

11. His handler, "Raul", was known to have organized crime connections; therefore, it was likely that the conspirators relied on a professional hit man. (A tried-and-true method, recalling how Hoover had insisted on them for the Kennedy murder.)

In conclusion, it is not possible to ignore the evidence that there was a widespread conspiracy to kill King and get him "out of the way". It involved a large spectrum of the Federal Government, particularly U.S. Army Intelligence, the FBI and the CIA, and likely even the Department of Justice; also, broad areas of the Tennessee government, such as the Memphis Police Department (MPD) and other local law-enforcement agencies, the state legal system and prison authorities. In a "matter" like that, multiple agencies and staff provide open or tacit support or acceptance.

The actual execution was contracted out to organized crime, as usual in operations of this type. In exchange, compensation was probably made in cash plus promises and concessions consisting in "laying off" and other hard-to-trace-or-prove actions or omissions. The government has ways of reducing or paralyzing persecution and prosecution of crime with pretexts of all sorts such as lack of evidence, security, general public safety, inadvisability, indefinite postponement, etc.

CHAPTER IX

The Strange Death of Vince Foster[8]

The presidency of the Clintons was a matrimonial enterprise, as evidenced by their effort to return to the seat of power eight years later[9] —and now, in 2016, just as this book goes to press—in a curious reversal of roles offering a startling gender-switch in the top executive position. Unmistakably, she is the one with the most brains, if far less charm and prevaricational skill.

Many analysts feel that the female side of this equation was the critical part mainly responsible for the election of her male partner. There is no doubt that Hillary was and is still a determined, highly ambitious political activist and strategist (although the years may have started to take a toll as evidenced by unusually weak and disconcerting statements made during 2014-16). Unable initially to defeat the bias against women in the highest office, she found a way to get to the pinnacle by marrying, advising and guiding a partner with the charm and slickness to make his way up the ladder, despite his amazing lack of intellectual prowess. Also, she had the smarts to realize that she could hardly compete with his political background as a state attorney general and governor, plus his slippery social skills, essential to get away with all kinds of shenanigans. Because he was so adept at the game, people have always found it easy to forgive and forget his faults.

What actually happened in the case of Vince Foster, for years a colleague and close friend of Hillary, is hardly knowable at this stage, much less provable. What we do know, however, is extremely disturbing. So much, that the American people have obviously preferred to NOT know about it. What they have picked up in sidelong glances is clearly too much—**far** too much for them to stomach. So, they have preferred to overlook, forget and ignore. After all, they elected the Clinton couple twice. It's hard to accept the possibility that anyone in the presidency,

---

[8] A top White House Assistant and close friend of President Bill Clinton and his wife Hillary, he was found dead in Ft. Marcy Park, a Virginia site overlooking the Potomac River near Washington, D.C. in 1992, within the first months of the Clinton administration.

7. See above.

[9] Also, 16 years later, after she was displaced by a relatively unknown candidate in the 2008 primary. At this writing, history is still in the making, and she is still a strong possibility to be back in the White House in 2017, this time running the show and not behind the scenes.

the highest office in the land, might stoop to that type of skullduggery. To do so would be, for the general populace, an admission of extreme stupidity.

Yet somehow, in ways mysterious, it appears the couple were involved in the "suicide" of this extremely intelligent and able attorney who was the backbone of the iconic Rose Law firm of Little Rock. One of the up-and-coming young female attorneys who joined that firm and came under his wing was none other than the wife of an extremely popular Arkansas politician who became the state's attorney general, shortly its governor for two (non-consecutive) terms... and later won the presidency—although not by a majority of the electoral college, but by a plurality (as a result of a third-party candidate who split the Republican and independent voters).

It is worth mentioning that another attorney who worked with Mrs. Clinton was Webb Hubble, rumored to have fathered the child that was brought up as their own by the Clinton couple. This has been discussed in Chapter I, Presidential Rapists.

If we look at the facts in the case it is hard to not reach a conclusion of high suspicion that something was not quite according to Hoyle. Since we are not in a court of law, where a judge can choose to reject evidence, arguments or objections, we have the right and duty to consider *any and all* arguments and aspects not necessarily admissible within the strictures of jurisprudence.

Although one should not be overly concerned with the personal lives of characters in this story, it is nevertheless important to look into such an area given that it is only human that affection, disaffection, attraction, rejection, and myriad other emotions have their bearing on events.

That the two, Foster and Mrs. Clinton, worked together very closely—perhaps closely enough to have maintained something beyond mere professionalism—has been established through public records and a number of books. One of them was written by Web Hubble, a close associate of both who went on to become chief justice of the Arkansas Supreme Court and later, due to a series of mishaps, mistakes and heaven-knows-what complications, served years in jail for corruption and misappropriation of funds in his custody.

Web Hubble's book, *Friends in High Places,* is a detailed autobiographical story of his experiences with Mrs. Clinton, her husband Bill and the whole clan at the Rose Law Firm in Little Rock; it tells us a great deal about what went on—by omission! In a book of 340-some pages, there is not a single word or innuendo that there was ever anything but a warm, friendly, professional relationship between the young Mrs. Clinton and Victor, or anyone else. (Was she so unattractive that she did not get even any admiring glances?)

Yet the book contains not a hint of anything to indicate that Foster and Hillary Clinton were aware that they belonged to different sexes— not even an innocent flirtation or dual-meaning remark. (Isn't that a normal occurrence between adults, regardless of marriage or other attachments?) Apparently we are to assume that they were just two sexless people, concerned exclusively with their professional activity and nothing else. That in itself leads to the suspicion that something is being held back.

Any measure of human nature tells us that individuals between puberty and extreme age are attracted to one another in more than a purely intellectual manner, regardless of any commitments such as marriage, engagement or other relationships. Therefore, it would have been perfectly normal for such an attraction to have existed between the two. Sexual or sensual attraction is not any kind of fault or misbehavior. It is simply a fact of life, and one must wonder why it does not show up at all in the book; in fact, it is not even so much as denied—denial being a round-about way of acknowledging a possibility.

The question is what *that* might have had to do with Victor's sudden, mysterious death. Perhaps nothing. Yet regardless of that, unanswered questions, curious circumstances and suspicious details are multitudinous.

The likelihood that the two were more than just professional associates, as we shall see, just *might* have had something to do with his death. Foster was doing extremely well in his law practice as the leading counsel of the Rose law firm in Little Rock and had little interest in becoming a relatively unimportant government official. It is only fair to say, however, that besides his possible relationship with Hillary, his close friendship since childhood with President Clinton might have weighed into the equation. In any case, what seems certain is that he was not looking to make any kind of career move.

So it is only reasonable to assume that he might have chosen to accept the appointment because Hillary had persuaded him to follow her to Washington, perhaps with the knowledge and encouragement of her husband the newly elected president. The "bimbo-eruptions"—as *she* called protestations by women sexually used or abused by her husband— which were well known in his home state, would no doubt only increase during his tenure as the powerful head of the executive branch. Perhaps Foster was being relied upon to take care of Clinton's wife while he, Bill, was thus free to pursue his womanizing hobby while disrespecting the dignity of the Oval Office.

The theory is worth pursuing, since it might help to explain the suspicious death of Foster, otherwise shrouded in mystery. In short, the scenario might have easily evolved according to time-honored tradition in terms of love/sex relationships.

In conclusion, there are too many unanswered questions and suspicious circumstances to justify the official verdict of suicide. Foster might have held himself responsible for the failure of certain federal appointments that he was in charge of vetting, and had reportedly been unhappy and at odds with the Clintons over "Travelgate", the controversial firing of the presidential travel office staff—not exactly under his jurisdiction. He also had an insider's knowledge of certain Clinton scandals such as Whitewater. However, it seems unlikely that professional troubles of that type might have triggered so extreme a response as to kill himself.[10] If the White House job was not to his liking, he could have simply tendered his resignation and gone back to the prestigious Little Rock law firm of which he was a major, highly regarded attorney. But first, a long list of inconsistencies, utter falsehoods, signs of an insistent, persistent coverup at the highest level and other facts that clearly point to something other than the official inquiry's conclusion.

1. Why, for example, would a suicidal human choose to jump in a car and drive from the office—a "safe" and convenient location where suicides occur in large numbers—**to a public place** where something or someone unexpected might turn up and deter him? What would be achieved by so doing?, other than complicate matters if determined to go through with it.

2. Are we expected to assume that Foster didn't say anything to his staff to excuse himself, such as "I have to run an errand and will be out of the office for a while"? Did he simply walk out without so much as a nod to anyone? No one appears to have ever been questioned about his last and final exit from the White House.

3. Although law-enforcement investigators were denied access to it, Foster's office *was* open to White House aides, who might have been able to remove or tamper with evidence.

4. No second autopsy was conducted, even though the first one was highly irregular and inconclusive.

---

[10] We do know from sources within the White House that on at least one occasion Mrs. Clinton apparently humiliated him with furious put-downs and criticism in front of the staff when discussing her health-care plan, which he had voiced some objections to. That this by itself might have propelled him to suicide, however, is hardly credible in a mature individual with too much experience and authority to allow himself to be driven to such an extreme by someone who was once a young professional under his tutorial supervision.

5. The photographs taken of the body when first located at Ft. Marcy Park, on a single roll of 35 mm film, were thrown out, allegedly because they were **said to have been overexposed**. Why weren't they saved for re-examination as evidence, just in case they could be restored?

6. Kenneth Star, the Independent Prosecutor in the case, was not the tough and no-nonsense professional he was depicted as. In fact, he was carefully selected by Attorney General Jeanne Renard to make sure that he would **go easy on the President and his wife** and not embarrass them in any way whatsoever. Among innumerable manipulations, irregularities and improper procedures, it is a fact that Star did NOT hand over **the initial handwritten notes** taken by investigators when first inspecting the scene. In all likelihood they were destroyed.

7. Foster's body looked so perfectly placed as to appear to have been deliberately staged. In a case of suicide by gunshot, the weapon normally flies off as the bullet is fired; yet it was found in his hand—which, by the way, **was not his dominant one** (he was right-handed, and the gun was in his left).

8. The handgun was a **.38 caliber**, which contrasts with a hole in Foster's neck, consistent with a **caliber .22.** Visible in a Polaroid photograph taken of him is a small hole in his neck, later dismissed as only a spot of "dried blood". (A bullet wound anywhere in the head is likely to produce a stream of blood, and hardly a single, round spot on surrounding areas such as the victim's neck.)

9. The fatal shot was in the vicinity of the mouth—an unlikely place for any suicide to point a gun, since the wound might not be fatal. That would defeat the suicidal purpose and lead to the sort of complications that any suicidal individual would dearly wish to avoid. (A wound in the mouth is **more consistent with a homicidal shot aimed at the head** but gone slightly astray, perhaps by an involuntary tilt of the head in an attempt to dodge it.)

10. Foster's fingerprints were not found anywhere except on the barrel of the gun. Which brings up a question: how does a suicide fire a handgun without holding the handle or pulling the trigger? (Sounds like, immediately after he

was shot, someone hastily **pressed Foster's fingers onto the barrel**, but missed the handle.)

11. There was very little blood on Foster's body or clothes, even though a shot to the head normally produces a considerable flow or stream. Neither was there brain tissue or bone matter to be found on the body, clothes or, above his head on the tree on which he was found resting. This is consistent with staging.

12. There was no soil or vegetable matter on Foster's shoes, as would be normally picked up by walking even a short distance on the trail to where his body was found. This clearly indicates that the death happened elsewhere and the body was **carried t**o the spot.

13. The FBI was left out of the investigation. The case was entrusted to the **Park Police**, an outfit that knows **nothing of criminal investigations;** additionally, it is under the control of the executive branch and subject to its control and instructions.

14. Family and witnesses were pressured to change their story. Foster's wife at first said that the gun found in her husband's hand **"was not his"**, since he owned "a silver revolver", quite different. However, certain influences must have been brought to bear, since she later stated flatly that **"it was his",** without explaining why she had changed her mind. By the way, the gun was found to be untraceable; if it did indeed belong to him, why would they not be able to trace it, find out where and when he obtained it?

15. Arkansas state troopers testified that Foster and Mrs. Clinton clearly had an intimate affair; they had witnessed regular encounters that could not be explained in exclusively professional terms. While an affair is of course not a crime, it does bring up possible motivations and cause-and-effect links in the case.

16. There was testimony from those who knew them that, in Washington, the relationship between Foster and Mrs. Clinton had suffered a breakdown, as evidenced by the fact that they were no longer on speaking terms. Such a situation would be extremely uncomfortable for people whose offices are in close vicinity and must necessarily

cross paths and coordinate activities. This brings up the **possibility of a jealous rage**, a trait of which there is some evidence in Mrs. Clinton's relationship with her husband over the years.

17. A suspicious car and individuals were seen around Ft. Marcy Park at the time the body was found. However, the vehicle was never identified nor were the individuals named; they were identified only as "**confidential witness No. 1" and "confidential witness No. 2**"; this was contrived under the guise of "not invading their privacy". Why would their privacy be of any concern? Were the "witnesses" somehow involved or privy to incriminating evidence that needed to be covered up? Furthermore, since prosecutor Star never put these witnesses under oath, they were allowed to change their story and contradict themselves to suit the conclusion sought by the investigators.

18. **No car keys were found in Foster's pockets or near his body**. (How did he drive out to Ft. Marcy Park?) However, the keys showed up later, in the hospital to which he was taken, as if someone had planted them there. (A reminder of the pristine bullet found next to John Kennedy's body in Parkland Hospital.)

19. Telephone records of calls made and received during the time of the event are missing. However, a close friend of the President, his wife and the victim, was heard calling Arkansas and reporting that Foster had died; this was **hours before the news was officially released**. Also, it is reported that a nanny working at the White House stated that she had knowledge that Foster had died two hours before the press release.

20. William Sessions, the FBI Chief at the time, **was fired** precisely at the time that Foster died. (What a coincidence!) If the Bureau was to be left out of the investigation, as actually happened, this might have been necessary in order to keep things under control.

21. The Park Police concluded the case was a "suicide" before even viewing the body, let alone starting an investigation. (It calls to mind J. Edgar Hoover's conclusion that "Oswald, and Oswald alone, killed Kennedy", 48 hours after the event.)

22. The story put out by the White House, published by the press at every instance, was that Foster "had been depressed" and had been prescribed a drug to improve his mood. The truth is that no one (his wife, for example) is on record with any such statement about his mental state; on the contrary, everyone interviewed said that he seemed perfectly normal during the days before his death. It was later determined that the drug was for insomnia and the prescribed dosage was so slight as to have little effect, even if taken during the day (instead of, as one would assume, just before bedtime).

23. A "suicide note" was mysteriously found in the bottom of Foster's briefcase (after it had been thoroughly searched) several days after his death; it had been torn into 17 pieces and **said nothing about killing himself.** (It complained about the pains and problems of life in Washington, but not a word about ending his life.) Furthermore, there were **no fingerprints on it**. How can someone write a note and leave no fingerprints? Why would anyone write such a note only to tear it up, and then—if that was a prelude to discarding it—drop the fragments where they would be easily found? (To be honest, that whole story is just too fishy.) Finally, no analyst was able to certify that it was Foster's handwriting. The conclusion is therefore inescapable: **someone else wrote the note to provide "evidence" of suicide.**

In conclusion, if Vince Foster's death *was indeed a suicide*, why did the government go to such an enormous effort and expense (no doubt several million dollars), not to mention unimaginable bureaucratic contortions, blatant untruths and distortions to conduct this obvious, egregious enterprise evidently designed to cover something up?

If it was *not suicide*, the unavoidable conclusion is that there must have been accomplices: President Clinton and his wife Hillary, of course, plus a considerable number of major and minor officials, not least of whom would be independent counsel Star himself. In that case, Mr. Star was not in charge of the investigation, but of the whole coverup of the homicide or murder that they got away with.

We shall let the readers reach their own conclusions.

CHAPTER X

Elián González,
a Child as Political Pawn and Victim

When the presidency of the United States—the executive power, that is—intervenes in a matter that is before the courts and uses brute force to take it out of the judiciary's hands and resolve the matter unilaterally, something is definitely awry. It reminds us of the recent use of "executive orders" (2009-2017) to circumvent the legislative branch, depriving it of its constitutional powers.

It is extremely surprising, not to say suspicious, that the judicial power let the matter ride out without so much as a peep of complaint. In other words, it accepted the unlawful action by the executive, thereby letting the child Elián González be sacrificed on the altar of what was most likely a blackmail payoff by the President of the United States.

But let us look at some actual, indisputable acts and facts. Why did the executive not let the courts exercise their constitutional duty to decide a case already before them? Answer: because, quite likely, the executive was blackmailed—yes, BLACKMAILED and given a deadline—to comply with the Castro regime's conditions: return the child to us by X date or suffer the consequences. And the executive asked the courts to downplay the issue, likely by alleging that if not, "national security" might have been affected. They had it backwards: **national security was affected** by the very fact that the executive got away with a senseless crime! —and further, deprived the judicial system of its right and responsibility to consider an issue and hand down its judgment.

So we have the Attorney General of the U.S. scurrying to send out a posse with assault rifles **in violation of law, justice and righteousness**, to attack a private residence in which a young child and his family could have been easily killed or injured, in order to KIDNAP said child, Elián González by name, and deliver him to a foreign oppressor.

Such an event should have been enough to impeach not only the President, but also the chief law-enforcement officer of the U.S., the Attorney General. That same President was later actually impeached and eventually disbarred for a much lesser offense—but that's another story.

Bringing together the pieces of the puzzle, they fit perfectly only if one considers the possibility of **BLACKMAIL**: information that, if revealed, might irreparably damage the presidency, bringing about the downfall of the Chief Executive and his whole administration. And it worked, as evidenced by the forcible handing over of a child whose mother had sacrificed her own life to get him away from the very same totalitarian regime that now demanded that he be turned over, or else.

By the way, *that* regime still has the power to demand and get whatever it wants from those subject to that blackmail: i.e., a couple who are still in the running to get back into the White House. Just imagine that scenario!

It bears mentioning that the presidential couple in question still has a lot of power over the press given that the possibility of blackmail has never been brought up—nor even hinted at—in connection with that case. Now **that** is a coverup worth noting, particularly when the destiny of the United States might hang in the balance.

So much for the free press!

CHAPTER XI

Lyndon B. Johnson's Sister

Something extremely suspicious happened to the sister of President Johnson, Josefa Johnson (1912-61), at a New Year's Eve party at his Texas mansion. The date of her demise was officially recorded in January of 1961.

This possible, unreported and unprosecuted felony seems unimportant in view of other crimes likely committed under his aegis, particularly that of the JFK assassination and the killing of over 50,000 Americans by going full-force into Viet Nam and transforming it into a tragic, international struggle fought at enormous human, logistical and financial sacrifices to the country. In case you are wondering why, the answer is GREED. The man profited immeasurably from under-the-table commissions paid him by the military-industrial complex that Eisenhower had warned us about only a few years prior. As a result, the Johnson fortune ballooned from close to zero when he was first crookedly elected to congress, to tens, perhaps hundreds of millions by the time that he was forced to give up running for re-election. He *could have* run, but 1) he was older and less energetic, and 2) he realized that the war that had made him wildly rich had also ruined his political career. And his appetite for the political arena had worn extremely thin. In short, he had had enough of the presidency.

In passing, it is worth noting that his fortune also received a huge boost when he arranged to transfer the space program to Houston, conveniently in his home state (the hands-on rocketry experts convinced him that the launching site had to remain in Florida; otherwise, that would have gone off to Texas as well).

Johnson's record in World War II, one of the many suspect episodes in his career, was carefully crafted. As a congressional representative from Texas since 1937, by 1940 he had been appointed lieutenant commander in the U.S. Naval Reserve. Three days after Pearl Harbor, he reported for active duty to the Chief of Naval Operations for instruction and training, after which he managed to be assigned to inspect shipyard facilities in Texas and on our Pacific Coast. Through connections with James Forrestal, Undersecretary of the Navy, he was assigned to a survey team of the situation in the Southwest Pacific, as a result of which he reported to General Douglas MacArthur in Australia. Johnson and two Army officers were assigned to the high-risk mission of bombing a Japanese air base in New Guinea. Johnson claimed that because his bomber somehow came under fire near the target (don't most bombers get fired upon under such circumstances?), it had turned around and flown safely back to base; others, however, reported that his aircraft was not fired upon but turned back due to generator trouble.

However, Johnson reportedly used the event to make a deal with MacArthur in order to get the Silver Star, the third- highest military medal, in return for which he reported to Roosevelt that conditions were deplorable and strongly urged higher priority and a larger share of war supplies to the region. Johnson's efforts not only helped with MacArthur, but they also got him named chairman of a high-powered congressional subcommittee on Naval Affairs. He had thus dodged danger and simultaneously boosted his career and prestige. So much for his war exploits, which he later used to good advantage when running for reelection.

Johnson's performance in the Senate, to which he was elected in 1949 after twelve years as a representative, concentrated on being an unprincipled sycophant of his party's leadership until he achieved his goal of becoming Majority Leader. He held that post fox six years until 1959, when **he blackmailed Kennedy into putting him on the ticket as the vice-presidential candidate**. Believe it or not, he ran for vice president AND for re-election to his Senate seat at the same time, thanks to legislative maneuvering that acted as insurance for whatever happened. (If elected to the vice presidency—as expected—he would simply resign his senatorial seat.)

That he also likely headed the conspiracy to assassinate President Kennedy is a monstrous crime still hushed, covered up and overlooked, despite all the evidence. However, it confirms the criminal nature of the individual still revered for his civil rights and "Great Society" achievements—the reasons for which were largely self-aggrandizing as well: he boasted that he had "won the black vote for the Democratic Party for the next 100 years". No one disputes that he must be given credit for such major advances, whatever his reasons. He made optimum use of grief over the death of his victim, President Kennedy, to push through Congress a series of bills that brought overdue equality to a large portion of the U.S. population. Those facts are not at issue and must be recognized as a major achievement.

Nevertheless, the fact remains that the possible murder of his own sister is but a sidelight that even the most careful biographers choose to ignore. We, however, will not. Let us proceed with the story, so quieted and unpublicized that one must wonder if it was nothing more than a faint pinprick within the context of his fabled career to the top governmental positions in the United States.

His sister Josefa Johnson fell ill, we understand, during this New Year's party, December 31, 1960, after which no one has any idea about what happened. We have located no reports, news items nor records of any type on the subject. It has to be surmised that, perhaps, after she suffered some kind of sudden ailment at this event, she was spirited away to a secluded room—so as not to disrupt the party—where she expired in due course: hours or days later? Someone with tremendous clout had to intervene, since we have been unable to uncover any information about the cause of her death, nor about what symptoms she had or where she was taken, if anywhere, for diagnosis and treatment.

Furthermore, we know of no investigation, autopsy or other effort by authorities or law-enforcement to find out why a mysterious death took place—particularly involving someone so closely related to a major political figure. Unless, of course, that figure chose to flex power in order to mute everything down to a whisper. Who would dare to stick out their neck when there was nothing to be gained but trouble? One might expect the powerful brother of such a victim to INSIST on determining the cause of her demise. However, nothing like that took place: quite the contrary.

The woman was likely an inconvenience. She had no children who might have been interested in her welfare or concerned about her fate. Word *has* filtered through that she was "loose" and therefore might have been an embarrassment to her famous brother. There!, was a probable motive for the callous decision to have her removed and buried, forgotten. Or perhaps there was another, more personal or familial dispute that got her into trouble.

But then, a man who kills 50,000 Americans for profit, plus assassinates a sitting president would have no qualms about taking out a close relative who was "in the way".

At this late date *we* have no means to ascertain the facts, nor do we have the wherewithal required to conduct any further, serious inquiry. The best we can do is write this with the hope that our story might stimulate readers who do have the wherewithal to conduct such an investigation and make an effort to find out the truth of what happened.

People who are unimpressed with the vast corruption and criminality of our subject might, at least, be humanly touched by evidence that he might actually have done away with his own flesh and blood.

CHAPTER XII

Castro's Drug-Smuggling Business Survives... by Executing Scapegoats

Few people paid any attention at the time, and by now fewer still are concerned about it.

However, the U.S. Government clearly had something in the works to retaliate against the Cuban Infidel for turning the island under his control into a base of operations for smuggling drugs into the U.S. By the 1980's the problem had become enormously expensive to control and repress, atop the huge damage to America in terms of addiction, untold suffering and general undermining of society—precisely what the Infidel wanted.

In other words, these were precisely the goals sought by the Cuban ruler: accumulating money for himself and financing his expansionist plans across the Americas, while weakening his preferred enemy, the United States. But the Infidel's highly efficient intelligence service learned that President Ronald Reagan was considering action against him, and he was going to take no chances. Reagan was not subject to the blackmail exercised by Cuba's totalitarian regime through its complicity and knowledge of the conspiracy and real culprits in the Kennedy assassination, so real danger lurked.

The Grenada affair, thought the Infidel, might be a taste of things yet to come. The American invasion, in 1983, put an end to the Castro take-over of the island's government, during which a runway capable of accommodating large bombers was being built under cover of flimsy excuses. The purpose, naturally, was to project power and threatening influence over the Anglophone Caribbean, plus Venezuela and Colombia.

The current American anti-Castro threat coincided with the increasing popularity of General Arnaldo Ochoa, a development interpreted by Castro as a danger to his regime. Ochoa had distinguished himself in Castro's armed intervention in Angola—a true imperialist ploy as opposed to the "American imperialism" that he railed against. Ochoa had become a popular figure in Cuba; there was, in fact, a secret longing that he might lead a coup d'etat and bring the country out of the retrograde autocratic nightmare established by the regime. In fact, graffiti saying "8A" (the number eight in Spanish is *ocho*) were mysteriously appearing throughout the country. But his domestic intelligence network was at least equal to his foreign one, if not superior. His spies were everywhere and Ochoa was being watched. Castro was wary and concerned that with broad support in the armed forces and the people at large, the general might have the power and, conceivably, the urge to overthrow him. Eavesdropping with hidden microphones revealed that he, Ochoa, was actually making plans to seize power with Tony de la Guardia, a top official, and a small group of their intimates.

"But what are we going to do about the old man?" said one of the recorded voices at a meeting of his conspiratorial group. Anyone who knew an iota about the Infidel realized that he was ruthless, devious and more dangerous than a venomous snake; therefore, the question was more on the order of "how are we going to kill him?" While Ochoa's reply was not recorded, we can be sure that it was not too favorable to the longevity of Castro. In fact, the presumed victim was already working on a plan to do away with Ochoa, just as he had done with everyone else who might have posed the slightest threat to his power and prominence. His response called for killing two birds with one stone. The concept, a master stroke, was simplicity itself: Castro would publicly accuse Ochoa of drug-smuggling—precisely what Castro himself had for decades been doing—while simultaneously cutting back on narcotics shipments through Cuba; this would demonstrate to America that he was serious about the drug problem and encourage U.S. officialdom to hold off any retaliatory action. The public trial and execution of General Ochoa, coinciding with a major halt—if only temporary—in the lucrative narcotics trade, would have a salutary effect on his own safety and the survival of his regime.

The trial was carefully arranged. Ochoa himself was encouraged to "confess"—no doubt to save his wife and family from the regime's tender mercies—and did so in front of cameras. He was most likely promised leniency on his family, and perhaps even on himself: why, they intimated that he might not even be executed! But he disbelieved these crumbs and acted like one who knows that his goose is definitely cooked. His testimony, judging from his recorded delivery, was not very convincing. He did not seem as sincere or repentant as they undoubtedly hoped for, but gave the impression of being forced to repeat words not his own. Further, there were some hints that he might have been given drugs aimed at mental and physical weakening, a standard procedure for totalitarian regimes conducting this type of circus. The accused is coached, threatened, reminded that his whole family's survival and well-being hangs in the balance, and then, just in case, given the precise pharmaceuticals required to erase any remaining resolve to resist.

The same held true about Tony de la Guardia, another top official who had always been very close to Castro. Somehow, Tony's twin brother Patricio was not executed but given a long prison sentence that he is likely still serving, if he has not by now succumbed to the mercies of Castro's political-prison prescription.

CHAPTER XIII

J. Edgar Hoover and his Private Bureau

The legendary Director of the Federal Bureau of Investigation, ensconced in a lifetime job full of perks and power from which no one—not even presidents—dared evict him on pain of all sorts of revelations carefully guarded in his secret archives, was confident that he would live out his days with impunity.

He had gotten away with all sorts of crimes and misdemeanors, among them cold-blooded murder, not to mention rampant corruption and autocratic rule that extended beyond his bureaucratic bailiwick with tentacles reaching into the legislative, the executive and the judicial branches of government. His word was law and no one was up to challenging him. The budgets he "submitted" to Congress were rubber-stamped and perhaps even enhanced with secret, under-the-table additions, well-disguised and difficult to trace.

Early in his administration, John Kennedy began exploring ways to "retire" him and put in his own man, in a broad effort to reorganize the Bureau, the CIA and other intelligence services. At one point he invited Hoover to come to the White House and confer with him and his Attorney General, Robert Kennedy, hoping to see if he could be induced to step down. No such possibility emerged: quite the contrary. The FBI head countered with hints that he had all kinds of sensitive information about the President's past and present activities, and would do "his utmost to make sure that none of it would ever leak out during his tenure". The brothers Kennedy strategically backed off and explained that they only wanted to find out about the Director's plans. Besides, they would see what they could do to provide additional support for him and his Bureau?

During the Johnson era things went along smoothly, as one would expect knowing that Hoover and the sitting president—quietly known as "the Usurper" within the Kennedy clan—were accomplices in the Kennedy assassination and thick as, well... thieves, in depredating and using the government for their own purposes. Hoover and Johnson had identical goals: basically to remain in power and put down any opposition that might threaten their position.

Eventually, Johnson overstepped his bounds by greedily raking in "commissions" from the military-industrial complex while cavalierly killing Americans in the contrived, wrongheaded and strategically useless Viet Nam war. Realizing that his family longevity was short and he might not be around much longer, he accepted his unpopularity and wisely chose retirement to his well-stocked, comfortable Texas ranch. After all, he had achieved his lifetime goal and remained president for a full term, elected in his own right after fulfilling the remainder of his victim's. Now, he would consolidate his legacy and engage in whatever activities would please him most.

The Nixon era would be different and perhaps perilous, Hoover realized, and prepared accordingly. Leaving his post into retirement would deprive him and his cohorts of power and position, and perhaps even open him up to all sorts of trouble arising from his crimes and corruption over nearly 50 years! His second-in-command, Clutch Towson, friend, confidant and lover, urged him to stay. Not ambitious nor especially healthy, Towson preferred to stay in the background; however, without Hoover he was concerned that he would soon be under bureaucratic attack, be demoted, or even pressured into retirement.

A practical man, Richard Nixon sent out his feelers to see what could be done about getting Hoover out without creating any trouble for himself. After all, he was well beyond the official age of retirement but refused to budge. There is evidence that Nixon feared Hoover because of certain information he might have been able to release on him, and on one occasion expressed concern that Hoover, if forced to resign, might "bring down the whole temple" with him. Prior to his presidency, Nixon had never been at odds with the FBI boss—they had been allies in the anti-communist movement—but now he was wary of Hoover and had one of his own men in mind for the Bureau. Hoover was not buying it; the perks of power were too valuable and the disadvantages of giving it up decidedly unattractive.

However, eventually Nixon tired of the waiting game and decided that the time had come to do something about the powerful FBI Chief. He called in his team of under-cover fixers, called "the Plumbers" because they frequently took care of leaks. Their boss was particularly upset by these leaks and the damage they did to his administration; the Plumbers dealt with problems of that type, as well as others that required secret action. At any rate, he told the team about his dilemma, and asked G. Gordon Liddy—a former FBI agent then on the White House "Plumbers" team—to prepare a psychological report on Hoover. Nixon judged the document extremely perceptive, and concluded that there would be fewer disadvantages than advantages to attempting Hoover's removal.

Incidentally, among the Plumbers' capers was the Watergate affair: the type of operation that required secrecy and, if revealed, deniability. While Watergate is a subject best discussed in a later section of this book, we will simply say that it had to do with the suspicion, played down for some strange reason, that the Democratic Party had received funds from Castro's Cuba. (That was the reason so many of those involved in the actual break-in operation were Cuban-Americans hoping to deliver a blow against the island's tyrant.) The idea was to expose the Democrats as having financial support from Castro and thus wield a major political advantage. As has been well documented, The Washington Trumpet turned it, a minor break-in in which nothing of value was taken, into a *cause celébre* and managed to orchestrate a coup d'etat.

At any rate, the Plumbers heard Nixon recite his dilemma and told him they would think about it and come back with a proposal within a few days. They offered then a plan to "take care of" the matter. Nixon started to ask what that would involve and then, wisely thinking that he was better off not knowing, backed off, saying "Wait—don't tell me. Just go ahead and do it."

We do know that within a few days, perhaps a couple of weeks, Hoover's housekeeper was suspicious when, early one morning, she had not heard him get up. Not up to walking in on him, she called for help. The police arrived at his well-appointed premises in one of Washington's upscale neighborhoods, went upstairs and found him lying in his bed, very still. It was odd that he was in his pajamas, since he usually slept naked.

Urgently called in was not, curiously, an emergency rescue team, but his doctor, who hardly needed to check on him before promptly pronouncing him dead. Upon further examination, the compliant physician said that he had died from heart trouble, even though Hoover had no history of it. He could not help but observe that he found his death surprising, since he had seen him recently and pronounced him in good health. Somehow, there was no further investigation into his demise, nor was an autopsy performed. Hoover's death was attributed to a heart attack brought on by age and that was that.

A magnificent, well-attended state funeral was held, with full honors and a wide range of officialdom present. His body was placed in the Capitol rotunda, and eulogies were delivered by President Nixon and others. Case closed.

We have since learned, however, that there might have been some foul play. Specifically, there had recently been break-ins into the Hoover house. Since there was little evidence of any disturbance and nothing had been removed, no action was deemed warranted nor taken. In retrospect that might have been a mistake of omission..., if not carefully pre-arranged.

While the federal government and that of the District of Columbia were very discreet about the whole matter and pursued no action that might have brought to light anything out of the ordinary, we have it from reliable sources that must remain anonymous that the break-ins had, indeed, something to do with what transpired.

While it was indeed true that nothing was taken, is it possible that something was brought in, very carefully and surreptitiously? What if a hypodermic needle was used to inject a toxic substance into a tube of toothpaste? What if the target brushes his teeth as usual before going to bed…, and never wakes up?

By the way, what if the housekeeper at some point became aware that something unusual was going on, during or after the break-in? Well, she could have easily been neutralized by telling her that they were conducting a routine check of security or other household equipment. "No need to inform the boss: he already knows", they might have said.

Mr. Hoover never had, that we know of, a recognized or formal heterosexual relationship—although he made it a point to publicly lunch with a few famous, attractive women at his usual, specially reserved table, in the Mayflower Hotel—for which, by the way, he was never billed a single red cent. The objective: to dissemble his sexual persuasion. Still, according to some sources, it is possible that he might have had a heterosexual affair or two: occasional bisexuality is characteristic of many primarily homosexual males, as well as of an even higher number of females. Because, during the 1940s and '50s, he was frequently seen with Ginger Rogers' divorced mother, it was rumored that at some point they might have been intimate. Although some have stood by reports that he cross-dressed at some homosexual parties, these are likely fabrications and out of character, since he was carefully protective of his image.

At any rate, he fathered no children and apparently left no familial heirs or close friends who might have inquired about his death under what might have been considered suspicious circumstances. His only sister died in childhood.

We do know that his Associate FBI Chief and intimate partner, Clutch Towson, inherited Hoover's ample estate and moved into his house. That would add credibility to statements by some that they had seen Hoover and Towson holding hands and, on one occasion, the director painting his friend's toenails when they vacationed together in a secluded, Mafia-owned retreat in California. The Mafia's certainty of his homosexual leanings—and consequent threat of exposure—might explain why he accepted the mob's offer of free vacation stays at some of their resorts, where he and his love-interest would be protected from prying eyes and enjoy themselves in seclusion. That would explain why he left the mob alone and repeatedly insisted that "the Mafia does not exist". He was only forced to abruptly switch directions when, in 1957, the top capos' meeting at Appalachin (New York State) was broken up by suspicions local police and made scandalous nationwide headlines.

The above ties in with stories about other bribes provided by the Mafia to Hoover: for example, tipping him off about winning horses in fixed races. The Chief, who loved the tracks, would go to the $2 window and place a bet on any nag, while a flunky would carry a briefcase with $100,000 at another window and place it on the winner. The couple also reportedly enjoyed the use of boxes owned and used by gays at the Del Mar Racetrack in California. Most of this sensitive information started coming out after Hoover's death, although writer and openly-gay writer Truman Capote loved to spread around whatever gossip he could about him. Capote's information was generally reliable and true-to-life—that's what hurt his friends and acquaintances, who mostly ostracized him when he spoke out and published their most intimate secrets.

On the news of Hoover's passing, just for insurance, Nixon named Towson as "inheritor" of the FBI captaincy, which he held for a brief period. This was confirmed by Nixon with the likely caveat that it was on condition that he leave the sudden death of Hoover well enough alone. A smart, discreet fellow, he probably felt—if he had any doubts whatever—that making a fuss would do him no good and cause him far more trouble than it was worth.

Again, case closed. The FBI headquarters, in downtown Washington, Pennsylvania Avenue, completed long after his death, proudly bears the name: "J. Edgar Hoover Building".

FOOTNOTE: Curiously, the biographical movie done Hollywood-style in 2014 or thereabouts by one of its long-time residents, Dint Westwood—the film is entitled "J. Edgar"—is a pure whitewash. Hoover is portrayed as a serious, hard-working guy who is not outwardly gay and devotes himself to fighting crime and communism. In his whole career as head of the FBI he never did anything wrong; he never had anyone rubbed out, never committed nor covered up any crimes or even misdemeanors, and never used his files to blackmail presidents, congresspersons or congressional committees; in short, he was a virtual saint whose purpose in life was to fight for justice, freedom and democracy, and to benefit all Americans regardless of race, creed, gender or socio-economic standing.

CHAPTER XIV
O. J. Simpson and Double Murder

All one can say about this case is that it was one of the worst miscarriages of justice in U.S. history—only in reverse. Miscarriages are usually understood to consist of punishing an innocent party for crimes not committed by the one convicted.

This went the other way: the exoneration of a murderer so clearly and completely guilty that it should have been an open-and-shut case.

Rather than going through all the ins and outs of the trial, the details, asides, arguments, objections, evidence, sidebars, etc., the process might be summarized by saying that it was a circus, a well-staged show. The prosecution pretended to put Simpson on trial while withholding evidence—enough, that is, to give the jury an excuse to declare him not guilty. The two prosecutors held back major pieces of evidence, or submitted them only in part and in such a way as to be unconvincing; they also let the defense get away with all kinds of shenanigans, among them openly racist tactics that had no place in a court of law. Behind the scenes, as we shall see, a secret, blatantly racist threat undoubtedly caused the two prosecutors to tremble and retreat. They did, however, have the effrontery to write a book purporting to tell the whole story of the trial in order to make themselves look like competent professionals who were somehow outmaneuvered by the defense.

The jury selection was another sham. Out of hundreds of candidates, those chosen had little education and were unlikely to have understood sophisticated procedures, chemical, technical and otherwise, designed to determine guilt. Nine were black women and as such more likely to sympathize with Simpson, rather than with his dead white victims. In the end, several jurors stated after the trial that they thought it likely that Simpson was the murderer, but attributed their verdict to mistakes in the prosecution's presentation and other deficiencies. Since when should prosecutorial mistakes allow a jury to let a criminal go scot-free? If jurors may take into account reasonable doubt and acquit, they can also override any and all prosecutorial errors if the evidence, as it was in this case, is overwhelming. It is their own opinion that counts above all else.

Clearly, something else was at work here. The prosecution made little effort to demonstrate the validity of DNA evidence proving that Simpson's blood was found at the scene of the crime as well as on the glove and the shoes he wore at the time. In effect, it allowed the defense to use technical arguments to belittle the fundamental fact that a suspect's blood at the murder scene is incontrovertible evidence. How did it get there if the suspect had nothing to do with the crime? Did he happen to be strolling by and witness the event without being at all involved? If that were the case, why didn't he call 911 and report it?

The defense's quip that "if it does not fit, you must acquit" is sheer nonsense. First, Simpson tried on the murder glove while wearing a cloth one to begin with—thus making it tighter—and second, anyone can twist and spread fingers in such a way as to make any glove appear too small. The way to check for fit is not by letting the accused try it on with stiff, twisted fingers, but by simply taking measurements or using a cast of his relaxed hand. How they let the defense attorneys get away with such claptrap is beyond anyone with a minimum of common sense. Clearly, the glove-fitting stunt was doctored to favor the accused and the prosecution should have not allowed it.

Then there was the chase in the Ford Bronco immediately after the killings. That was not brought up at all by the prosecution. Why would an innocent man attempt to elude police? Why, Simpson's friend Al Cowlings, who was driving, even said that Simpson had a gun pointed to his own head during a considerable part of the chase—which, by the way, lasted one hour and a quarter and involved dozens of police cars and helicopters! Again, fleeing from justice is simply absurd for someone innocent. But was that brought up at the trial? Absolutely not. Furthermore, the prosecution also omitted any mention of what was found in the Bronco: a passport, several thousand dollars in cash, and items of personal disguise. Why, if innocent, would anyone pack such items unless attempting or planning to get away, perhaps to another country. And why take flight in the first place, instead of showing up at the nearest police station to clear up any suspicions.

The prosecution moved the trial to Los Angeles instead of keeping it in Santa Monica, where it should have been held, since that was the jurisdiction in which the crime was committed. Could it be that L.A., with its large black population, would be more favorable to the defendant? Nothing was to be gained prosecutorially by this change of venue, chosen on the excuse that it would provide more "security". Why would security be an issue? Would the local citizenry, composed mostly of peaceful, law-abiding families, rise up in arms to protect an accused assassin?

Simpson's bumbling alibis that 1) he "overslept" the night of the crime and did not leave the house, 2) he was practicing golf in his back yard, and 3) he was taking a shower, all at the same time, sound so phony that a six-year-old would laugh at them. He also gave differing, conflicting explanations of how he had cut his finger and thus stained the blood-soaked glove that was brought into evidence. We have already dealt with the absurd demonstration to falsely show that "it did not fit".

Not only was there proof that the left-hand glove—and its right-hand companion, located in Simpson's house—belonged to him, but there was also conclusive evidence that the footprints found at the scene of the crime were matched by the unusual, very scarce Italian shoes, Bruno Magli brand, in Simpson's own size, that he regularly wore. What else did they need, a photograph of Simpson knifing his victims to death?

Incidentally, a knife salesman testified that he had sold Simpson a 15-inch, German-made knife similar to the one used in the killings. In case you are wondering, that should have made it premeditated, first-degree murder. However, he was not charged with that; in fact, the prosecutor alleged that Simpson had attacked Michelle and her companion in "a fit of jealous rage". That is a lesser offense, subject to a less severe penalty. At any rate, the prosecution discarded the death penalty and requested life imprisonment, no doubt to reduce the jurors' burden if they managed to find him guilty.

Incontrovertible proof that Michelle had been the victim of spousal abuse was ignored, even though there were pictures of black-and-blue marks on her face. Michelle Simpson had made a 911 call on January 1, 1989, asking for help and protection against her husband; she not only expressed fear that Simpson would harm her, but in fact his yelling was clearly heard in the background during the call. Also, evidence that Simpson had recently taken a Navy SEAL course in preparation for a TV series, was dismissed—even though, as part of the course, there was a picture of him holding a knife to a woman's neck! (Did that give him any ideas?) The prosecution's excuses for not using it were that such a photograph might have been "too graphic" and "staged". What?

Further, Michelle Simpson had also filed complaints that her (by then) ex-husband had lately been stalking her, and was afraid for her life. Michelle stated that Simpson had warned her that if he ever found her with another man he "would kill her". But was that significant fact submitted as evidence of motive or intent during the trial? Well, er, no.

Finally, if Simpson didn't do it, who did? Did anyone ever come up with any other likely suspects. Well, er, no.

The major question was why was this sham perpetrated, enabling a killer to get away with a bloody, premeditated double murder. The answer is that Johnny Coburn, the lead defense attorney, likely threatened the prosecution and the authorities with a repetition of the **Rodney King riots** unless Mr. Simpson was **found not guilt**y. Racism at its worst. Otherwise, how could one explain the fact that the judicial process turned out to be completely subverted?

His own worst enemy, Simpson eventually did himself in by breaking-and-entering and stealing items having to do with his career, but no longer belonging to him. Clearly, he is a career criminal who thought, since he had gotten away with murder, that he was above the law and could commit other crimes at will and likewise go unpunished.

A civil suit filed by the families of the victims was decided in their favor and resulted in a judgment of $40 million in damages, the court concluding that Simpson was likely responsible for their wrongful death. But the families are unlikely to ever receive a single cent, since Simpson moved to Florida, where a homestead exemption blocks creditors from taking one's residence; besides, he took other measures to hide and/or protect the rest of his assets.

Listed below are some of the curious details concerning this case that practically screamed out Simpson's guilt, although not enough to convince a prejudiced jury. He was not only responsible for a double murder, but also of orphaning his two helpless children.

☐ DNA analysis of the blood found in, on, or near Simpson's Bronco showed traces of Simpson's, Brown's, and Goldman's blood.

☐ DNA analysis of blood on the left-hand glove, found outside Brown's home, was proven to be a mixture of Simpson's, Brown's, and Goldman's.

☐ DNA analysis of socks with blood stains found in Simpson's bedroom proved that the blood was Brown's. Since the blood stains made a similar pattern on both sides of the socks, the defense medical expert testified that such a pattern could result only if the wearer had punctured his ankle or someone placed a drop of it on the sock while not being worn. In short, he argued that the socks might have been contaminated during processing, an event so unlikely that it strains credibility far beyond the breaking point.

☐ Stars of African-American hair were found on Goldman's shirt. If so, it should have had it analyzed to see if it matched that of Simpson.

☐ The gloves contained, in addition to blood, particles of hair consistent with Goldman's, while Simpson's cap contained carpet fibers consistent with those found in Simpson's Bronco. A black knit cap found at the crime scene contained strands of African-American hair.

☐ Several strands of dark blue cotton fibers were found on Goldman, who according to a witness were similar in color to a sweat-suit worn by Simpson that night.

All of this evidence—a smoking gun if there ever was one—was obviously more than sufficient to convict Mr. Simpson of first-degree double murder.

A miscarriage of justice indeed.

CHAPTER XV

Rigged Elections

It's not the number of votes that   count;   it's who counts them.
— Josef Stalin

Hayes-Tilden, 1876

In this presidential contest, Republican Rutherford B. Hayes was declared the winner over Democrat Samuel J. Tilden, who had won the popular vote. It was a dispute so intense and topsy-turvy that Louisiana, Florida and South Carolina came up with two sets of differing electoral-college results, one in favor of Republican Hayes and another for Democrat Tilden. Eventually, the election wound up in the House of Representatives, where a special committee was created to decide the matter.

Accusations were made against the Democrats in the South for violence and threats against blacks—whose vote favored Republican Hayes—thus boosting Tilden. On the other hand, there were allegations of fraud against the Republicans on voting results that put Hayes ahead in the North, so the two charges in a way offset each other.

The special committee's membership was supposed to be evenly distributed: five Republicans, five Democrats, and five Supreme Court justices; of the latter, two were from each party and one, David Davis, was an independent. However, since Davis had just been elected to Congress, he resigned his appointment to the committee, as a result of which a Republican was designated in his place. The resulting membership was therefore unbalanced: 8 Republicans and 7 Democrats.

In the end, in what was called the Compromise of 1877, a deal was made in Congress under which Hayes agreed to withdraw all federal troops from the South, ending the Republican reconstruction, in exchange for awarding him the disputed electoral votes. According to the initial electoral college count, Tilden had come within one vote of being president—he had 184 and needed only one more to reach the winning number, 185.

Tilden's conduct during the whole process was passive and disappointing to his supporters. While the Republicans claimed victory, Democrat Tilden mystified his own side by not actively rallying his advocates nor providing any leadership. He instead spent over a month researching a century of electoral college procedures, apparently to demonstrate that the decision-making body was not the Senate, but the whole Congress. That was totally ineffective and seemed to seal his fate. He continued to be active in politics but failed to win his party's nomination for the next presidential election.

In conclusion, it has been demonstrated not only that elections are subject to fraud and corruption at the local and state level, but also at the federal level, where the so-called electoral college can be subject to manipulation, influence-peddling and other shenanigans. In fact, its members have even been known to make up their own mind and vote for their preferred candidate, regardless of who they were actually supposed to vote for according to results at the polls.

Was Tilden threatened or intimidated, or was he temporarily affected by a mental disorder?

Truman-Dewey, 1948

It was billed as the "big upset". But guess who really won the election. I know, the sitting president had a lot of sympathy and support. But why did the New York Times headline say "Dewey Beats Truman"? Well, that's what **all the polls** said, so anything different would have been extremely unlikely. As we all know, surveys are often a more accurate reflection of popular feeling than actual voting results, affected as they are by fraud, impersonation, double and multiple voting, "resurrection" of voters long dead, miscounting, threats, bribery, coercion, and uncounted other shenanigans. On the other hand, those asked for a personal opinion have no reason to deceive anyone, since they don't count as an election.

Truman was a not-too-outstanding haberdasher from Missouri, picked by Roosevelt for the same reason as his other running mates— they were politicians who had hardly been heard of. One of them, John Nance Garner, famously complained that the vice-presidency was not worth "a bucket of warm spit". They were all relative unknowns and would not overshadow him as the center of attention. Oh, Truman did a creditable job of handling the government when he inherited most of FDR's fourth term, which had hardly begun. However, he was a same-party successor and after 16 years of Democratic control Americans wanted a change in the White House. The Democrats had enjoyed an inordinately long run in the presidency, and it was time to hand over the reins.

Dewey was an extremely popular figure, a top prosecutor against organized crime in New York, no less, giving him a major platform to run on. His integrity and capability having been demonstrated against the Mafia, the underworld was dead-set against him. His level of education and effectiveness, his organized and disciplined mentality, were far superior to Truman's, who was considered a hack from the corrupt

Prendergast machine controlling Missouri. After spending his youth on a farm, Harry Truman saw service as an Army Artillery officer toward the end of World War I, and upon returning set up a haberdashery—the reason he always had "haberdasher" attached to his name. But while in the service he had befriended Tim Prendergast, a nephew of corrupt political boss Tom Prendergast, who had been running the state for decades. The connection proved useful when Prendergast, on a recommendation from his nephew, picked Truman for an administrative judgeship; young Harry was grateful and played along, and the die was cast for greater things. He went on to become a senator in 1935 and made something of a name for himself in congress as a military-spending reformer. Harry was loyal, sharp and tough, and won reelection to office despite Prendergast's decline into disgrace. FDR took notice and somehow, in declining health, observing Truman's dependability, chose him as his running mate in the 1944 election. Taking office a few months after Roosevelt's fourth inaugural, Harry inherited the presidency while knowing little about the intricacies of the wartime government. He actually did a creditable job despite a reluctant Republican congress, overcoming many obstacles in a difficult era: he stood firm in the cold war against the Soviets and showed guts in the hot war in Korea.

In the domestic arena he used his executive power to abolish discrimination in the Armed Forces and seek other, less controversial reforms. But he held no brief against the Mafia and had taken no particular action against them. On the other hand, as indicated above, Dewey had made a name for himself by fighting against them tooth and nail.

There it is, in a nutshell. The Mafia had solid reasons to intervene on Truman's behalf. Since they did NOT want to be persecuted and prosecuted by Dewey, the best way to avoid that was by denying him the top position. Truman, on the other hand, was reliably opposed to pursuing the Mafiosi; in fact, he made sure to lay off and keep them on his side. There is no way to prove that he planned it that way—except that a book on Sam Giancana's life written by his sons Sam and Chuck— entitled *Double Cross*—so indicates, and the story rings true. It makes sense that, from the Mafia's viewpoint, there was no way that Dewey would be elected if *they* had any chance of stopping him. The surprising result, contrary to all expectations, went uncontested by the "loser", for who knows what strange reasons (perhaps similar to the ones in the Kennedy-Nixon case, ten years later). Dewey curiously chose to concede and close the books on that chapter.

Kennedy-Nixon, 1960

America is still feeling the effects of this electoral fraud fifty-some years in the past. Defeating the collective will and intelligence of the American people has consequences far beyond those apparent at the time of any deed.

As we now know, the Democrat-controlled, Mafia-enforced system established in Chicago, turned the results upside-down in Illinois and fraudulently gave that key state to Kennedy. Together with a similar operation in the Johnson fiefdom of Texas, the Nixon victory was subjected to a complete about-face and turned into a defeat. It is well known that Johnson was an expert at fixing elections, starting with the one that launched his career with a roar: his very first contest. Even though the press and the establishment have long been covering up all this wrongdoing, time has a way of bringing up the truth and we are at last learning something about what really took place. Books dealing objectively (as opposed to still-prevailing rampant idolatry) about JFK's life and administration—such as *The Dark Side of Camelot,* by Seymour M. Hersh, 1997—reveal a veritable wealth of long-suppressed information that explains the mysteries behind the foreign policy disasters of the period. Much has been written about LBJ as well, but it has been overwhelmingly favorable. If anything could be described as not exculpatory—i.e., harsh truth unvarnished—nothing has been as devastating as *A Texan Looks at Lyndon – A Study in Illegitimate Power,* by J. Evetts Haley, Canyon, Texas, 1964. It is too bad that, thanks to efforts by Johnson himself and his followers, this book had extremely limited circulation and today is nowhere to be found. The historical events discussed therein, with a wealth of detail, show unquestionably that its subject had excellent motivation to suppress its circulation.

As to Nixon, why did he not bother to contest the election? As above indicated, the reason was simple: he was likely threatened by the Mafia, the very same group who had fixed the result for JFK. After going to that trouble, why on earth were the Mafia going to let things get out of hand? Foreseeing the possibility that he might demand a recount, they had prepared a response. Oh, it was not that Nixon himself would be in danger—he might have stomached that—but that someone "close to him" might suffer an accident or unspecified endangerment. *That* did it. Nixon bowed out overnight. He was still young enough to run again and become the nation's leader—and so he did eight years later. On the other hand, asking for a recount 1) would have been too dangerous, and 2) might have yielded the same rigged result. Eisenhower did not bother to weigh in on this or anything remotely related. His mind was always on the golf course anyway and the sense of responsibility on his shoulders had already worn him down to the point at which he was through, **by**

early in his first term, with the rough and tumble of politics. He preferred to remain aloof and above it. Curiously, he never cared much for Nixon anyway, and he likely consoled himself with the thought that the nation would be in no danger with a Kennedy presidency.

Well, how wrong that turned out to be! I refer you to the chapter on the Bay of Pigs disaster, attributable exclusively to JFK's weakness in the face of blackmail. Nixon would have **doubled down**, not *backed down*. The failed invasion brought on the Missile Crisis and the 57-year Castro reign of terror within Cuba and throughout Latin America... which is still ongoing (despite its now dormant appearance, what with the renewal of diplomatic relations and all such window-dressing).

If you are wondering what "evidence" there is to prove the above, I must tell you that I have read practically all the books written by the Mafiosi of the era and their descendants—*All American Mafioso* (re Jake Rosetti)*, The Silent Don* (a biography of Santo Trafficante), *Double Cross* (ditto, Sam Giancana), *Little Man* (ditto, Manny Jalonski)—and they all, directly or indirectly, tell the same story: a crooked deal was made between Sam Giancana, the *capo di tutti capi*, and Joseph P. Kennedy, the Patriarch of the Clan, whose key words were: "Guys, you give my son the election, and our family will lay off yours".

As we have later learned ("suspected" for the squeamish), the beneficiaries of the Mafia fix reneged on their part of the bargain and double-crossed them. The result was the murder of John F. and, five years later, of his brother Robert. [11] Three decades later, as have seen in this book, it was John, Jr.'s turn to make the final journey.[12]

Bush-Gore, 2000

This election, the winner of which was declared to be George W. Bush, was another highly questionable contest.

Considering how close the vote count was in Florida, and primarily because that state's electoral votes would decide the election, Albert Gore was quite right in calling for a recount, and then two more. (It is quite likely, not to say evident, that he was never threatened, the Mafia having had no stake in this election.)

Since the outcome, still by a thin margin, was basically unchanged after two recounts, the call for an unprecedented third one brought about a lawsuit that went all the way to the U.S. Supreme Court, which refused it. The Secretary of State of Florida then certified George W. Bush as the winner according to the original result, unchanged after two recounts.

---

[11] See the author's book, *Getting Away with Murder—and Costra's Crimes—In U.S. Public Life,* amazon.com, 2013.

[12] See the latter part of Chapter III.

It is quite likely that the Supreme Court, with a majority of justices appointed by Republican presidents, was inclined to side with that party and thus decided against further recounts, in effect adjudicating Florida's electoral votes to Bush. Also, it should be kept in mind that Florida's Secretary of State was a Republican appointee. Admittedly, the unprecedented third recount might have gone too far and thrown the country into prolonged instability. It stands to reason that the final result might have been unduly influenced, considering the possibility of a different vote count.

The question remains, however, of how many recounts can reasonably be requested after two confirming the same original result.

Obama-Romney, 2012

Any informal survey taken by an average citizen will reveal an unspeakable truth: the re-election of President Obama in 2012 was, and remains, one of the most suspect vote-countings in recent American history.

Let us give him a clean electoral victory in 2008, even if based on the ingenuous nature of the American people, who collectively thought that putting a black man in power would end once and for all the notion of "racial discrimination" in American life—a serious domestic and international-relations problem. It sounded like a simple, magical solution. Also, they expected in would greatly smooth out distrust among human groups of diverse ethnic origins, domestically and perhaps in the world at large. But his re-election after four years of lackluster performance, atop his suspicious "executive actions", coddling of certain groups and suspect leanings with regard to muslims, well... let us say that we're hardly convinced that things were exactly what they seemed. Like him, we believe in respect for the Muslim faith and all others; it is only the extremists that we are concerned about, although we have not honestly seen enough action to demonstrate concern on his part.

That said, let us state that electoral shenanigans are one of the oldest methods designed to foil majority will. The procedures used are as diverse as the human mind can devise: deliberate and "accidental" miscounting, switching of digits and totals, deficient arithmetic, false representations, outright fraud, etc. These days, computers can be easily programmed to yield any desired result; therefore, their use is no guarantee of honesty—just the opposite.

It is simply not credible that Obama cleanly won the key states required for an electoral-college victory. He was far less popular than when first elected and had demonstrated too many weaknesses in foreign policy, while his domestic governance was clearly disastrous. "Obama Care", for example, was and still is an utter economic and health-system failure passed by political juggling against the overwhelming majority of the public and enacted by a cowed and outmaneuvered Congress. Just the enormous bureaucracy required to manage—or perhaps mismanage—it would make it possible, perhaps, to provide free health care for those whose dire needs it was supposedly designed to alleviate.)

The above electoral conclusion does not even take into account possibilities of fraud in other states such as Illinois, whose Mafia-controlled machine is centered in Chicago—Obama's political base. It is a well-known fact that the electoral machinery in that state has a way of turning elections around—for example in the Kennedy-Nixon contest, dealt with elsewhere in this chapter.

But let us consider only the four states in which the election was decided by a margin of less than 4%, a degree of closeness sufficient to be tampered without any consequences to speak of (clearly, larger differentials are more difficult and dangerous to overturn). These states and their respective margins of victory for Obama were: 0.88% in Florida, 2.04% in North Carolina, 2.98% in Ohio, and 3.87% in Virginia. Now, taking the aggregate 75 electoral-college votes for these four states, let us simply switch the Obama total of 332 vs. the 205 for Romney: the result turns the election around; 280 (205 plus 75) for Romney and 257 (332 minus 75) for Obama. It doesn't take any degree of genius to appreciate that the Obama supporters might have figured out in advance the close states and taken the necessary measures to put them in his column.

Furthermore, if a poll were taken today of those who voted in those states, it would yield a result contrary to the one presented as official and trustworthy in 2012. Even assuming that a majority of black and Hispanic voters in those four states favored Obama, it is likely that there were more than enough Romney supporters in the rest of the population to offset such a margin. The general, non-black and non-Hispanic population group, heavily anti-Obama, has traditionally registered to vote in far higher proportions and has been much more likely to go to the polls. These votes likely far outnumbered, in most key states, those cast for Obama.

But thanks to the media—to America's misfortune an autocratic, one-sided, agenda-driven system populated by professional "members of the club"—i.e., the like-minded—the results of the 2012 election, far from being questioned, will not even be discussed for perhaps decades to come. It is, of course, far too late: challenges must be brought immediately in order to bring about a recount. Such a process would not necessarily be honest and above-board, but certainly would have been worth a try.

But have you ever wondered why losing candidates—even though they should file for a recount, rarely do so? There is a reason: those who have rigged the contest usually threaten them with consequences if they contest the result. Although those consequences might not affect them directly, they might be dangerous to their family: "accidents happen, and your family might not be safe", they say. That is usually more than sufficient to bring about second thoughts. The game, as the saying goes, is not worth the candle.

In brief, the results of the 2012 election were quite likely fraudulent. The winner was not Obama, but Romney.

CHAPTER XVI

Jimmy Hoffa's Last Words

"They wouldn't dare." So said James Riddle Hoffa, the former tough-guy Teamster boss and now ex-convict—thanks to Attorney General Bobby Kennedy's lifelong efforts and "Get-Hoffa Squad"—when he heard that the Mafia was planning to finger him to be hit when he persisted in attempting to get back his job as head of the Union.

That was the fearless remark of the man of whom RFK at one point observed that "he thinks he's more powerful than the U.S. Government". Hoffa and Robert Kennedy hated each other's guts so intensely that once, when in an elevator, he called him a "spoiled brat" to his face and started after him (Hoffa was a powerful weight-lifter, proud of his physicality and capable, during his days as a union organizer, of taking on guys twice his size). But Frank "the Irishman", his right-hand man, wisely held him back. Hoffa eventually reached a point of hatred at which he lost his self-control, called his underlings in charge of "straightening things out" and told them: "BOBBY'S GOT TO GO". He meant that as an order to do a hit on him.

He rescinded that order only when he checked with his Mafia pals, who told him that they were planning, instead, to do away with the President himself. If Bobby were hit, they reasoned, JFK would "unleash the dogs" on them: therefore, the target should be the "Prez" himself and not his brother. Carlos Marcelo, Hoffa's pal and boss of New Orleans, quoted the Sicilian adage, "If a dog bites you, cut off its head, not its tail." What was Hoffa's reply to that?: "Well, what're you guys waiting for? You've got my full support."[13]

Word somehow got to "the Prez", JFK, that Hoffa, surprisingly, was planning to rub out Bobby. Little did JFK know that, a short time later, the union leader would switch targets and be in on the conspiracy to wipe out him, the President of the United States himself. At any rate, JFK took Washington Post editor Ben Bradlee aside at a White House soirée and whispered to him what he had learned. "The Prez" —as his family called him—knew that his brother Bobby was reckless enough to take no self-protective measures—he used to drive around in a

---

[13] Hoffa got his wish. The mob, as executioner for the conspiracy, got them both—and Hoffa got to enjoy that, even though when RFK was hit he was in the Lewisburg penitentiary, doing time as a result of Bobby's prosecutorial efforts throughout the years. When the President was assassinated and RFK was Attorney General he suspected Hoffa of being implicated, but concluded that he was not the main culprit. (See *Getting Away with Murder—and Costra's Crimes—In U.S. Public Life;* also Chapter II of this book.)

convertible all by himself—and wanted Bradlee to make the story public to provide him with some protection. But Bobby found out about it and begged Bradlee to spike it, explaining that it would discourage witnesses scheduled to testify against Hoffa. *That* was more important to him than anything else.

Not that Bobby was a saint, either, since he could have been disbarred for a number of unethical actions, use of unauthorized wiretaps, bugs and other illegal activities. It is also said that RFK, who was prone to violent outbursts, committed acts of violence against prisoners and detainees. However, as we now know, the worst of his actions have been well covered up by his still-loyal friends in the press.

Backing up to before the 1960 election, when Hoffa got word from top capo Sam Giancana that the Cosa Nostra had decided to make sure JFK got the presidency, Hoffa said "no way!" He would have none of it, no matter whose decision it was. Accordingly, the Teamsters Brotherhood International was the only labor union that went for Nixon in the face of the Mafia and the AFL-CIO's decision to back Kennedy. But Hoffa's support was not nearly enough. As we know, John F. Kennedy "beat" Richard Nixon by a "razor-thin" margin. The truth was that the mob made sure to RIG IT by "counting" enough Kennedy votes in Chicago to offset Nixon's plurality in upstate Illinois. They did the same in Lyndon Johnson's Texas and thereby locked up the election. Just in case, they threatened Nixon into not calling for a recount, not by advising him that "something might happen" to *him*, but to members of his family.

Hoffa was absolutely sure that "old-man Kennedy"—meaning clan Patriarch Joseph P.—who was Giancana's friend and associate from Prohibition days, would never be able to control his kids and keep them from pursuing the Mafia. But Giancana, a close friend of Frank Sinatra and other Hollywood types who were pushing for Kennedy, would not listen. They took the bait, and were then smacked with the punishment when RFK started after them big-time as soon as he took office.

But back to our story: the hit on Hoffa, the hard-driving, tough- as-nails union boss who had come up through the ranks had made all kinds of corrupt, illegal deals with his friends in the Mafia. He had turned the Teamster's huge pension fund into an endless source of capital for building casinos in Las Vegas and Cuba, while pocketing lucrative commissions for himself under the table.

Hoffa's right-hand man was one of the few Mafiosi who was not Italian, but Irish. In fact, Hoffa called him "The Irishman" and made him into his top hit-man, available at a moment's notice to "straighten out" a matter: rubbing someone out in Mafia lingo. The mob never referred to killing as doing a "hit", as they say in the movies; instead, they "straightened out" a problem or, if they chose to use a threat beforehand, the code phrase to the potential victim was "that's how it is".

The first words heard by Frank "The Irishman" Sheeran when Hoffa telephoned to hire him on the recommendation of one of his Mafia pals, were: "I hear you paint houses". In Mafia-talk that refers to rubbing out someone, considering that the act might splash blood, i.e., "paint", over the walls.

No slouch, Frank quickly replied: "I also do my own carpentry work", another code phrase meaning that he got rid of the bodies. It goes without saying that the Irishman spent perhaps a decade or so travelling throughout the country doing "jobs" for Hoffa, "straightening out" matters and giving "that's how it is" advice to those who might be stepping out of line. Besides that, he had played a part in the JFK assassination by supplying three high-powered rifles to the snipers in charge of the crossfire that made his head explode from multiple dum-dum bullet impacts. The closest he would come to talking about "Dallas"—as they referred to it—was remarking that Hoffa and Carlos Marcello would warn him not to discuss it whenever they sensed he might be bringing it up. One never knew who might be listening.

Frank "The Irishman" Sheeran, during his fifty-some-year career as a mobster while collecting two salaries from the Teamsters and all kinds of "juice" and "vig" from loan-sharking and multiple other rackets, had met and dealt with the top capos in the business, from Chicago's Sam "Momo" Giancana to New Orleans' Carlos Marcelo, to Philadelphia's Russel Bufalino, to New York's Joe Bonanno and Meyer Lansky, to New Jersey's Tony "Pro" Provenzano, to Tampa's Santo Trafficante and Hollywood's Johnny Roselli. He had also dealt with and passed instructions to lesser known but key operatives such as David Ferrie—Carlos Marcello's pilot—and Jack Ruby, who ran two night clubs for Marcello in Dallas and was assigned the Oswald rubout.

"The Irishman" also had had contact with high-level politicians such as John Mitchell during his tenure as Nixon's Attorney General, and Joe Biden, whom he judged to be favorable to the Teamsters; therefore, he arranged for contributions for his initial bid for election as senator from Delaware, as well as for subsequent re-election campaigns.

In trouble with rival Mafiosi a couple of times, "The Irishman" survived by being smart, never "ratting" on anyone and playing the "loyal and reliable" card no matter what. He followed orders and "straightened out" with bullets at close range any number of targets assigned to him, such as Joseph "Crazy Joey" Gallo. One might say that Gallo got his just desserts, since he had been assigned to rub out capo Joe Colombo, who was calling too much public attention to himself and the Cosa Nostra by creating an Italian-American Foundation. However, in a violation of protocol, Gallo shot him in a public place and in front of his family.

Worse, he bungled the job by failing to kill him, turning him instead into a vegetable for a number of years. "The Irishman" also rubbed out other high- and mid-level Mafiosi, including, as we shall see, his closest friend and mentor.

But Hoffa trusted him with his life—a mistake in the Mafia world. Jimmy was living a life of ease and great wealth, but he most enjoyed the power. He exercised it most ostentatiously from the "Marble Palace" or "Palace Hotel"—as they called the impressive headquarters building put up on Capitol Hill by the International Brotherhood of Teamsters, within sight of the Capitol itself. However, by virtue of his corruption and criminal activities with his partners in the Mafia, he provided Bobby Kenned and the Justice Department with plenty of ammunition against him. Thus far he had beaten them all: fraud, attempted bribery, jury tampering, etc. (Although he had ordered numberless hits, the prosecutors never had enough evidence to prosecute him for murder.)

But eventually prosecutors brought an air-tight case that he was unable to shake off. Hoffa got sentenced to 13 years for blatant jury tampering. He exhausted the appeals process and was sent to Lewisburg penitentiary. Despite the sentence he remained president of the Union and continued to run it, as best he could, from behind bars. But since that was not easy, he had to name his best buddy Frank Fitzsimmons as "interim" union head while he "went to school", i.e., did his time in prison. Except that Fitzsimmons was much nicer to the Mafiosi than Hoffa; so the mob concluded they would stick with the "Fitz" in the event that Hoffa ever got out.

Sure enough, it wasn't long before Nixon, who was grateful for Hoffa's dedicated support in his political life, decided to pardon the labor boss. It didn't hurt that Hoffa arranged to deliver hefty sums—on one occasion $500,000 in a satchel, hand-delivered to Nixon's Attorney General John Mitchell by Frank "The Irishman"—as contributions for Nixon's re-election campaign.

By this time RFK himself—who had been the original target instead of his brother the President—had been hit by the mob before he could even get to the nomination, let alone the presidency.[14] Not only did that hit make Hoffa happy—his air-tight alibi was being in the penitentiary—it made the pardon a lot easier. There was no one to make a fuss about letting his getting out of jail.

It did not matter that one of the conditions of the pardon was that he refrain from getting back into labor-union work. He would get around that by filing appeals based on the fact that a pardon with conditions was

[14] See Chapter III of this book and Chapter XXX of *Getting Away with Murder—and Costra's Crimes—in U.S. Public Life.*

an unconstitutional violation of his rights to engage in his regular activities that enabled him to make a living.

The pardon had been structured in order to keep Frank Fitzsimmons as president of the Teamsters and keep Hoffa away from the Union even longer than if he had stayed in jail another year or two.

Hoffa swore he would find a way to get even with Fitzsimmons, "the traitor" and with Charles Colson, a Nixon operative whom he blamed for the conditional pardon. He was quite capable of doing that, since he was just as ruthless as any mob members. He had demonstrated that by having his enemies killed, maimed and even blinded by throwing acid in their eyes—as happened to Victor Reisel, a labor reporter. (No one was ever prosecuted for the crime: instead, witnesses were threatened or killed). Hoffa's strong-arm tactics were legendary in taking over and controlling the locals and the national Teamsters union, and he was preparing to use them once again to have his way.

Ah, nice plans! But the big Mafia bosses weren't too happy. They were quite satisfied with Fitzsimmons and he with them, and they weren't going to let Hoffa spoil their honeymoon. So when it was clear that James Riddle Hoffa meant business about getting his job back, they were nice enough to not rub him out forthwith, but give him notice that "that's how it is".

Hoffa was so outraged that instead of wising up and backing off he blurted out "They wouldn't dare!" It never occurred to him that if they dared and succeeded in getting him out of the away it would be game over.

Frank "The Irishman", his right-arm man, was chosen to set him up. That's how the mob always does it. They don't hire a stranger to do it; they "ask" one of the victim's best friends to do it. That way, the victim lets his guard down and never suspects what's coming. Although Frank did not know it, the plan called for rubbing *him* out too: by eliminating the killer, he can't talk and reveal who put him up to it. But at the last minute a friend decided to spare him and Frank was able to dodge the bullet.

The upshot was that Frank "The Irishman" and several other men stopped by to pick up Hoffa, presumably to take him to the Machus Red Fox, a local Detroit restaurant. Since Frank was among them and had often acted as Hoffa's trusted bodyguard, he felt safe enough. "They wouldn't dare", Hoffa was still likely saying to himself. But he never got there. Although Frank had always insisted that he was called off the hit at the last minute, eventually, some thirty years later—he was in his 80's, an achievement for any mobster—he had to confess to a close friend and get it off his chest. "I pulled the trigger", he said, "because I had to."

Afterward, we have learned that they took his body to Bagnasco's, a funeral parlor owned by mobsters, and cremated it, then scattered the ashes. At that time in Michigan it was no problem at all to legally cremate a body, no questions asked. All they needed was a piece of paper called a "transit permit", no bigger than a dollar bill. And even that was sometimes dispensed with if a small bribe passed hands.

Hoffa's former pals in the mob were not satisfied to "take care of" Hoffa himself. Because he wouldn't listen, they also punished the family. They had told him "that's the way it is" and he had chosen to ignore the warning.

"Listen, Jimmy", one of his friends told him, if they killed the President of the United States, why wouldn't they kill you?" Perhaps he was still delusionary, thinking of the back-handed compliment that Bobby Kennedy had given him by implying that he was "more powerful than the U.S. Government".

He should have known better.

But how did they punish the family?, you ask. Well, just in case losing Jimmy himself weren't enough, by making the body disappear his loved ones can't collect any insurance for a long time. In this case, it took seven years before Hoffa was declared legally dead. To this day his remains have never been found.

They did a top-notch "paint job" on his house.

CHAPTER XVII

ASSORTED COVERUPS IN BRIEF

To get this book into the public domain before the November, 2016 election is of the essence. Americans should be informed about recent history before they make another mistake in their choice of leadership. That priority requires treating the following cases superficially, since conducting deep research and thoughtful sifting of antecedents and evidence would put off the printing date considerably, perhaps years down the road. Consequently, there is no choice but to summarize them now in the hope that at some future time, I or another author will be able to flesh them out more fully. For now, it is important for my readers to know at least something about them.

John Wilkes Booth Got Away with It

The supposed death of Lincoln's assassin, one of the most famous actors in America at the time, was trumped up to allow him to escape. According to underground information—mostly discredited by the press and other reliable sources for 150 years and counting—he got away scot-free and made another life for himself under the name "John St. Helen" in a remote Texas village, where he was practically unknown. It is said he lived on under this name and others that he assumed until his death in Oklahoma, into his nineties.

If we examine the circumstances in which Booth was supposedly located and shot, in rural Virginia, a number of suspicions arise. For example, why wasn't every attempt made to capture alive anyone suspected of murdering the President?[15] That would have made it possible to question him and identify any conspirators. The existence of accomplices was unquestionable in view of Booth's easy get-away, attempts by his accomplices to kill other high government officials—mostly unsuccessful—and the intense hatred of Lincoln by Southern sympathizers, many of whom openly vowed revenge.

Was it necessary to set fire to the barn where "Booth" was holed up? Or to shoot him as he attempted to escape the fire? Of course not!

---

[15] This brings up a comparison with Oswald, framed for killing JFK, who was then promptly executed so he could not talk. See Chapter III, The Kennedy Brothers and Their Conspiratorial Enemies.

The surrounding forces could have compelled him to give up or, in any case, waited for him to run out of food and water and surrender. The troops should have been under orders to **make every possible effort** to capture and avoid harming him.

The coroner, on inspecting the body submitted to him as Booth's, is said to have remarked that there was so little resemblance that he was not sure that he could ascertain that it was actually that of the famous actor. However, since he certified that it was indeed Booth, the suspicion arises that he might have been persuaded to do so by an outright bribe or a threatening statement such as: "We need your certification, sir, that this is the body of John Wilkes Booth. National security requires it. Is that clear?"

The fact that the family apparently identified the look-alike "Booth" in his casket is easily explained if we but consider that they would have wanted him to be thought dead so that he would not be caught and executed.

Once "dead and buried", Booth was free to get lost in a territory where he would not be recognized: initially, Texas. Another, perhaps paramount advantage was that he would not be questioned; thus, the top conspirators would remain unknown. That is, no doubt, why none of them were ever identified.

As a matter of fact, evidence exists that Teddyerson Davis, who presided the Confederacy, deposited funds in a Canadian bank to finance the conspiracy against Lincoln, which included paying off Booth and the actual executioners. Although the conspirators were to have killed Lincoln months or even one year before, they went ahead with their plan after the Union victory as an act of revenge for Lincoln's devastation of the South.

The conspiracy managed to control events so carefully and minutely that, as a result, only the minor accomplices were arrested and prosecuted for the president's murder. Curiously, they were tried by a **military tribunal** instead of a regular civilian court. Why? Obviously a martial court is more apt to be under control, harsh, free from the strictures of proof required under civil jurisprudence and notoriously prone at the time to impose the death penalty.

Sentenced to death and hanged were a few underlings: Lewis Powell, a conspirator who, on instructions from Booth, attempted to kill Secretary of State William Stewart (who was wounded but survived); George Atzerodt, who was instructed to kill Vice President Andrew Johnson but failed to even attempt it, and John Surratt, a rebel agent who collaborated but did not participate in the actual deed.

The fourth victim, also hanged, was an innocent woman, Mrs. Mary Surratt—John Surratt's mother—whose only involvement was running a boarding house where some of the underlings stayed. Was that a crime? After sentencing her to death, five of the jurors signed a letter requesting clemency for her and sent it to Lincoln's successor and then president, Andrew Johnson. He apparently dismissed the petition but later evaded responsibility by claiming that he had not received it. (Accused of corruption later on, Johnson was the first president ever impeached, the effort to depose him failing by a single vote.)

Meanwhile, John Wilkes Booth, the assassin and leader of the group of executioners, was "dead" and could not be questioned. How convenient!

A book entitled *The Lincoln Conspiracy*, published in 1977, detailed a government plot to conceal Booth's escape and gave rise to a film with the same title. Attempts by the Booth family to conduct DNA tests on his remains and thus settle the matter have been blocked in the courts, leading us to wonder why.

Are the conspirators' descendants, among them the Booth family, still working on the coverup?

Lincoln's Defeat
Stephen A. Douglas—famously of the Lincoln-Douglas debates—was a powerful politician and extraordinary orator who pulled out all the stops to win the senatorial seat from Illinois in 1858—absolutely ALL the stops. He used fair means **and foul** to rig the election and defeat Abraham Lincoln for that prized position, a springboard to the presidency.

However, in the general election for president in 1860, Lincoln earned the Republican nomination and turned the tables; he handily defeated Douglas, the Democratic candidate. Lincoln's persuasiveness and heartfelt generosity must have worked a charm not just on voters, but on Douglas, who despite his loss was conciliatory and supportive, and actually attended Honest Abe's inaugural at the still-incomplete Capitol building.

The Truth About the Emancipation Proclamation
The burning question of whether Lincoln mishandled the relationship with the South, causing the death of hundreds of thousands—more than in all other U.S. wars combined—and widespread destruction throughout the southern region, is a question buried under the praise heaped upon Lincoln after his untimely demise. True, he signed the Emancipation Proclamation to free the black race from slavery; but it was a maneuver during the Civil War to outflank the South and make it difficult for the rebels to prosecute hostilities by taking away their property, i.e., their rights over blacks. The slave-holding states were the enemy and located mainly in the South. The Proclamation was an executive order issued by Lincoln on January 1, 1863 to change the

federal legal status of over three million enslaved people in the South, making them free. As a practical matter, when slaves escaped the control of the Confederate government, either by their own initiative or thanks to advances by Union forces, they became legally free. Although eventually it reached and liberated all of the slaves, at first it did not, affecting only the slaves in ten states. Under the President's war powers, it had to exclude areas not in rebellion; therefore, it covered about 3 million of the 4 million slaves then extant. It was not a law passed by Congress, but by the president's constitutional authority as commander in chief. The Proclamation also ordered that, among those freed those who qualified could be enrolled into the U.S. Armed Forces. Further, the Union Army and the whole federal government was to "recognize and maintain the freedom of" the former slaves.

It should be noted that the Proclamation did not outlaw slavery nor did it compensate the owners of the freed individuals; furthermore, it did not grant citizenship to the ex-slaves. It only made it a specific goal of the Civil War to eradicate slavery throughout the country and reincorporate the Confederate states into the Union.

Few now realize that the Proclamation applied only to slaves in Confederate-held areas, and not at all to those in the slave states not in rebellion: Kentucky, Delaware, and Missouri —not named—; neither did it apply to Tennessee, unnamed and occupied by the Union troops since 1862, nor to lower Louisiana, also under occupation. Also excluded were those counties of Virginia soon to become the new state of West Virginia.

As part of Lincoln's plans to subdue the South, three months before the Proclamation, on September 22, 1862, the president issued a preliminary warning that he would order the emancipation of all slaves in any state not ending its rebellion against the Union. Since none of the Confederate states responded, Lincoln signed and issued the order on January 1, 1863.

The Emancipation Proclamation outraged white Southerners and their sympathizers, who were concerned about a race war. It also angered Northern Democrats, energized abolitionists and undermined European plans to help the Confederacy. Specifically, by making the abolition of slavery one of the two primary war goals, Lincoln deterred intervention by Britain and France.

In any case, the Proclamation encouraged the African-American population, both free and slave, and moved many slaves to escape from their bondage and get to Union areas to secure their freedom. It officially expanded the mission of the Civil War, since Lincoln's initial goal had been to maintain the Union.

The Emancipation Proclamation was never legally challenged. But to ensure the abolition of slavery in all of the United States and its territories, Lincoln managed to get the Thirteenth Amendment approved by Congress and ratified by the states on December 6, 1865.

As we know, a tragically assassinated president gets great press, as proven some 100 years later by the JFK case. Critics of Lincoln remained silent and, instead, glorified him for preserving the Union and freeing the slaves.

But has it occurred to anyone that the **Union might have survived perfectly well** if the states had been left alone to decide their own affairs? In due course, slavery was obviously destined to disappear without the need to fire a single shot. Therefore, "preserving the Union" was, at best, a false pretext for four years of slaughter and destruction.

The Watergate Scandal: Little-Known Facts

It is little known that the burglary was actually committed by exiled Cubans and Cuban-Americans (for example, Virgilio Martínez was a bona fides Cuban and Bernard Barker was a Cuban-American) who were hoping to discover that the Democratic Party had received funds from the Castro government. Should proof of such a transaction have emerged, a case might have been made for U.S. action against Castro. Thus, the "burglars" were motivated to feel that it was their patriotic duty as Cuban-Americans to go through with the caper. Another interesting note is that they were also trying to find out about a reputed call-girl ring run from the Democratic Party offices, which if proven would have been a political bombshell.

In a word, there is more than meets the eye to the Watergate affair, which was really a coup d'etat by the Washington Post, a journalistic near-monopoly that has had a partisan bias since time immemorial. Republican Party leaders, down to Barry Goldwater, conducted a shameful retreat in the face of the newsprint and media barrage against the President, making it impossible for him to stay in office. Other chief executives in recent memory—you know who they are—have engaged in far worse behavior with little if any consequences.

Antonin Scalia: a Mysterious Death

The death of this Supreme Court Justice in March 2016, is extremely suspicious. It took place at a Texas ranch belonging to a Democrat, a friend and supporter of the president, where Scalia was not protected by a security detail, a fact known to those interested in ending his tenure on the court. Further, his death was certified by a Justice of the Peace who had not even seen him, but learned of the event by telephone and magically pronounced that it was due to a heart attack. The official who reported it said he "saw no evidence of foul play". Questions: why did he feel compelled to say that?, and how did he reach that conclusion without investigating? Accounts of how he was found stated 1) that he had a pillow over his head (did someone smother him?), and 2) that his sheets were "unwrinkled". These two points are *extremely* disturbing. No investigation was conducted and no photographs were made of the scene. Finally, no autopsy was authorized nor performed.; thus, the cause of death was not officially determined.

The question is: why was there not an autopsy? Since when is it standard procedure to NOT do an autopsy on the suspicious death of a top-ranking government official? Further, any death whatsoever—let alone a VIP—that occurs outside of a hospital is a coroner's case and requires an autopsy. If not, in this case the judicial branch itself, not to mention the executive as well as the legislative power, should INSIST that it be done, just to eliminate any possibility of foul play. It seems odd, to say the least, that no such thing happened. Even if, due to religious qualms, the family does not accede to the autopsy—there is no certainty that they objected in this case, although we do know that grieving relatives are subject to suggestion and pressure—they have NO RIGHT TO PREVENT IT. When there is any possibility of homicide or murder, regardless of how slight, matters of faith do not prevail over established rules and regulations.

What does this all lead to? I will tell you. What if an earth-shattering case comes before the Supreme Court prior to the end of the current president's term? And what if that case has to do with his successor as Chief Executive?

If the justices are in a four-to-four deadlock, there is no judgment and the case is referred back to a lower court. There, pressures are more easily applied to ensure the desired outcome.

The Latin phrase *cui bono*? (who profits?) is pertinent here.

Jorge Mas Canosa: Death by Induced Cancer

A top leader of Cubans in exile, Mas Canosa escaped the Castro regime in early youth and, after coming to the U.S., became an extremely successful businessman. Concerned about the oppression and official anti-American stance in his native Cuba, he established the Cuban-American National Foundation (FANC) in 1981 in order to channel efforts within the U.S. to oppose the Castro brothers' tyranny.

Among other achievements, the FANC was instrumental in getting the Reagan administration to create TV-Radio Martí, a broadcasting facility designed to inform Cubans about news and information banned by the regime-run, strictly controlled media on the island. The Foundation was also active as a powerful political action committee in support of freedom and human rights.

After the Soviet Union collapsed, Mas Canosa hoped for change in Cuba. Although disappointed, in the mid-90s he was lured to visit high officials of the Russian government who seemed willing to discuss the Cuban question.

Did he get anywhere with the Russians? Of course not. It was most likely a trap.

Why was it a trap? Well, not long after his trip to Russia he came down with lung cancer.

Why is that suspect? If you read Chapter VII, "Exit Hugo Chávez After a Job Well Done", you will find the solution. When someone is in the way, cancer is easily induced by subjecting the target to intense radiation, generally under the bed. And then, "Oh, too bad! He got cancer!"

So you see, the Russians—and Castro-Cubans—are experienced in administering lethal doses of radiation to those they want to get rid of.

Let us not forget other possible victims—this time within the U.S.— such as Jack Ruby, who was hired by the JFK conspirators to kill Oswald, and James Earl Ray, who was framed for killing Martin Luther King, and likely also killed by induced cancer

Jorge Mas Canosa was a patriotic American citizen most likely killed by Castro skullduggery because of opposition to his completely legal, democratic and above-board activities. What did the U.S. do to investigate his death or bring up the matter in a diplomatic or international context? Absolutely nothing.

Enough said.

Oswaldo Payá Sardiñas: Death by "Accident"

Another peaceful citizen murdered by totalitarian masters for attempting to relieve the people's lack of freedom and human rights.

Brought up in a Catholic family in Cuba, Payá was the only student in his school who refused to join the Communist League after the Revolution. He served a three-year hard-labor sentence for a minor infraction of rules. While a student at the University of Havana he was harassed and expelled simply for being a practicing Christian. He persevered, however, and eventually made a career as an engineer for a surgical-equipment government enterprise (the regime being the single and only employer).

In 1992 he attempted to run for political office, but was not allowed to do so (he might have won and embarrassed the authorities).

Offered an opportunity to leave Cuba during the 1980 Marilynl boatlift, he opted to stay and work for a change. He founded the Christian Liberation Movement (CML) in 1987 in order to help free political prisoners and promote civil liberties. He also published an unofficial Catholic magazine calling for Christians to lead the struggle for human rights, until the regime forced the Church to clamp down on it.

While raising a family with three children, he began the "Varela Project", a campaign to collect 11,000 signatures which, according to the regime's new constitution, made it possible to call for a national referendum. It was the country's most important peaceful initiative to seek change in the totalitarian government, and gave Payá international recognition as an advocate for progress and human rights.

As one might expect, the top authorities in the regime accused Payá of being an agent of U.S. imperialism hoping to destroy the achievements of the Revolution. But he struggled on and in 2002 managed to collect over 11,000 signatures, plus 14,000 more in a second-stage effort. The petition called for a referendum on safeguarding freedom of speech and assembly, private business ownership and an end to one-party rule. In a visit to Cuba, former president Jimmy Carter gave a televised address in which he advocated the referendum, thus bringing it to the attention of a broad popular audience within the island and internationally.

As a result, the European Parliament recognized his efforts and awarded him its prestigious Sakharov Prize for Freedom of Thought. Payá managed to obtain an exit permit from the regime and, in months following, met with Pope John Paul II, U.S. Secretary of State Colin Powell and Mexican President Vicente Fox to promote the cause of democratic reform in Cuba.

Again, as one might expect, the Varela Project was rendered ineffective by the regime, which used its own power and devices to block it. As if Payá were hazardous to its health, when the dissident leader had actually supported many of its official demands, such as lifting the U.S. embargo—particularly on food and medicine—and not backing or receiving aid from Cuban exiles in the U.S. Furthermore, in 2005 he also had a public disagreement with a well-known democracy activist, accusing her of working with the regime's security to set the scene for a crackdown on dissidents.

Although his political activity was not attacked by the regime on those few occasions when they let him travel abroad, Payá stated that he was subject to routine intimidation, as was his family: "I have been told that I am going to be killed before the regime is over but I am not going to run away."

Payá was tireless. He continued to struggle, petitioning the regime, eventually under the Infidel's brother Raúl—when it became a hereditary monarchy—to provide for multiparty elections, free political prisoners, and allow freedom of travel. Nothing dangerous or violent about that!

Once Payá's brief period of international recognition as Cuba's Foremost Dissident began to fade, the government felt it safe to act against him. It arranged for a traffic "accident"—a method of elimination that the regime was experienced in thanks to years of practice. Confirming this, a reporter for "Foreign Policy" commented afterward that "Ramming vehicles carrying dissidents and foreign supporters, including diplomats, has been a stock-in-trade act of intimidation by Cuban state security for years."

A heavy truck was assigned to follow Payá's sedan and ram it from behind at a timely moment. Payá, age 60, was killed by the impact, as was the chairman of the CLM's youth league, Harold Cepero. There you have it: two birds with one stone. Accompanying these men were two sympathetic politicians, one from Sweden and another from Spain, who received minor injuries; the authorities forced them to testify that the crash was accidental. However, they later recanted and told the truth: the truck had rammed them not once but SEVERAL times and eventually forced their sedan to go off the road and crash into a tree.

And these are the people that the U.S. Government has been coddling and cozying up to since 2014! Friends, accomplices and supporters of North Korea, Iran and Russia!

I rest my case.

The "Suicide" of Washington Post Owner Philip Graham

Early in 1963, powerful media mogul Philip Graham is found dead in his bathtub from a shotgun blast. Separated from his wife for a considerable period, he was living with his mistress, Robin Webb, in a comfortable house where they gave dinner parties and invited important and prominent guests.

The media mogul had become so estranged from his wife Katharine that he had made successive modifications to his will, now in its third "edition", at this point leaving nothing to her and everything to his mistress. So she was about to lose the newspaper—which had actually belonged to her father—and very nearly everything else, except perhaps for the house where she had lived with Graham and their children.

Born in South Dakota (1915) but raised in Miami, Florida, where his father did well in real estate and farming, "Phil" Graham was very bright and extremely enterprising. An Air Force intelligence officer during World War II, he went on to Harvard Law School, where he was editor of the Harvard Law Review and earned a *magna cum laude* degree. A half-brother, Bob Graham, was a senator from Florida and his college room-mate, George A. Smathers, became state governor.

Never one to miss an opportunity, he married the daughter of multimillionaire Eugene Meyer, who eventually was named head of the World Bank and made Graham editor and publisher of the then-struggling Washington Post.

In the political arena, Graham was close to the Kennedys and Lyndon Johnson as well, and recommended to Kennedy that he take Johnson as his running mate. At times, his ability as a writer caused both men to ask him to write speeches for them. By then in his mid-forties, he was wealthy, well connected and extremely successful.

But he had his problematic side. He was fond of alcoholic beverages and began showing symptoms of mental disturbance. Having gone to Arizona with Robin Webb—an Australian journalist who had become his mistress—to a newspaper convention, he made a series of shocking remarks while addressing the gathering, among them mentioning that John Kennedy was involved in an affair with Mary Pinchot Meyer, known to be the wife of CIA agent Cord Meyer. (That detail was not published by The Washington Post nor by any other newspaper, there being at the time a "gentleman's agreement" to respect the private lives of public officials.)

Whether he was under the effects of alcohol or a mental problem was not clear, but he was diagnosed as manic depressive (what is today known as "bipolar disorder") and flown back to Washington, where he was taken to a psychiatric facility in Rockville, Maryland. After repeatedly asking the doctors to let him stay a few days away from the facility in the care of his wife—who said that he was "noticeably much better"—the two went to their Virginia farm for a weekend. Yet, according to the sketchy information reported on the event, Philip Graham suddenly killed himself with a 28-gauge shotgun. Conveniently, his wife was said to have been in another area of the country retreat.

If he was "much better", why would he take his own life without any warning or even hints that he might have been considering such a drastic measure? There was no indication that something like that was on his mind. If so, he would most likely have mentioned it to someone such as children, his mistress or even his wife. But there was no sign at all of anything of the kind. If he was known to be mentally unstable, why would anyone leave a deadly weapon in his vicinity? (At any rate, if it comes to ending it all, there are more humane and efficient means, such as sleeping pills.)

Was it a coincidence that he had just concluded yet another modified will that completely excluded his wife?

Well, guess what. It did not hold up. Not the last one nor any of the two previous ones in which he had gradually left out his wife. His own attorney, Edward Bennet Williams—a high-powered Washington personality—persuaded the courts that he, Philip, was not of sound mind when he had changed his will, even though he had made three successive "editions" of it in a row, all very carefully edited and witnessed under his own care. Well, you might ask, why did Williams agree to draw up these new "editions" for him? According to Williams—also a close friend of his widow Katharine and now *her* attorney—because he was trying to "humor" him. (Yeah, right! How much did Katharine pay him for these special post-mortem services?)

In brief, Katharine Graham inherited the newspaper and everything else that—according to a prior will—she and her husband had accumulated before they had split up and he had moved out. Certainly, the "suicide" of Philip came at the timeliest possible moment.

As you may have guessed, the power of Edward Bennet Williams and that of Mrs. Graham—particularly in the expectation that she might inherit The Washington Post and the entire fortune—held sway and surmounted any and all barriers. We are left to wonder if Robin Webb, Philip's mistress, received some undisclosed compensation to cause no further trouble. It is curious that nothing was ever heard from her again. Yes, you read that right: a prospective heir to millions, as designated by Graham in his last three wills, was left without one cent. Hmmm.

And the authorities, in their own mysterious ways—under who knows what undue influence or pressure—found it appropriate to close the matter by declaring Mr. Graham's death a suicide, despite evidence that made it unlikely, or at least highly suspicious.

Did Katharine Graham—or more likely, someone in her employ—find a way to "take care" of her husband before more time went by and it might become too difficult to contest the latest will?

It may be noted that The Washington Post reported NOTHING that might imply anything contrary to the story that Philip Graham had killed himself and was not of sound mind when he had revised his will for the last time.

* * * * *

These last words were
written in Leesburg, Virginia
on September 15, 2016

www.ingramcontent.com/pod-product-compliance
Lightning Source LLC
Chambersburg PA
CBHW060627290526
45793CB00001B/175